For Bill, ANYTHING

For Bill, ANYTHING

Images and Text for Bill Berkson

EDITED BY JARRETT EARNEST AND ISABELLE SORRELL

Pressed Wafer | BROOKLYN

PRESSED WAFER
375 Parkside Avenue
Brooklyn, New York 11226
www.pressedwafer.com

ISBN: 978-1-940396-10-1
FIRST EDITION
Printed in Canada

JARRETT EARNEST

Preface · *The Divine Conversationalist*

> And
> Always embrace things, people earth
> sky stars, as I do, freely and with
> the appropriate sense of space. That
> is your inclination, known in the heavens
> and you should follow it to hell, if
> necessary, which I doubt.
>
> —FRANK O'HARA,
> *A True Account of Talking to
> the Sun at Fire Island* (1958)

I was lucky enough to catch Bill Berkson at the very end of his twenty-five-year tenure at the San Francisco Art Institute, taking his last seminar, "Personal Culture." Structured along the themes of Italo Calvino's *Six Memos for the Next Millennium*—"lightness," "quickness," "exactitude," "visibility," "multiplicity," and "consistency"—the course moved gracefully through analyses of everything from Balanchine to Balenciaga, Dante to Edwin Denby. Toward the end of the semester he handed me a slip of paper, a quarter of a page with the titles of twelve books written out in his easy hand: "Here's your reading for about the next ten years." At first I misinterpreted it as "required reading for the general art student," but now I see it—both the gesture and the list— as a portrait of Bill Berkson and his generous way of engaging with the world.

George Eliot's *Middlemarch* was included, so I brought it with me to the banks of a lake in North Carolina that summer. The noonday sun liquefied the spine of my paperback. I saw this melted book symbolically, since I was also caught in the fervor of my first great love. Several disparate experiences became wedded by means of an emotional glue, the way things can be when they happen all at once: *Middlemarch*, young love, water-skiing, Bill Berkson and his reading list. I began to write passionately in my journal about how physical longing feels; how language can't keep up with feelings; and how George Eliot's compassion smelled of freshly baled hay. I wrote some of this to Bill, enclosed photographs and drawings, and put the letter in the mail. I soon received an email saying we should meet up for lunch when I was back in town. He went on: "What you are working through seems a lot like what O'Hara was doing at Harvard, so reading his *Early Writings* (especially the 1948 journal) and then his substantial poems of later years (from 1952 on) might be a time saver." I followed this advice, we did meet for lunch, and the conversation has gone on from there to the present.

I share this account because it highlights an important aspect of Bill Berkson: he is an ideal interlocutor, someone whom other writers and artists treasure having conversations with. He sets people, ideas, and things into unfailingly insightful dialogue. As both poet and critic, Berkson is dedicated to openness, to keeping our idea of the world available for new and as yet unimagined excitements. (Think of the name of the magazine he published: *BIG SKY*.) By recording the surprises he encounters moving through this big world, he lets us join in on his fun. Watch how he explores the expanse of a Poussin landscape:

> Letting your imagination wander through the depicted space, you see clearly the address of figure to figure, figure to dramatic incident and all of those to the registers, across the painted cloth, of landscape and weather, and then, after all that, the address, in the way of unfolding, of the whole picture to you as you look, as you look to comment on it, or listen, to whoever is looking alongside you at the same time, too. It's not that the paintings are simply conversation pieces, but you feel the beauty, order and passion generated from talk and mutual contemplation.

The freedom offered by Poussin's painting resonates with Berkson's philosophy of art writing, which shares his experience of looking as it connects to ever broader modes of thought. He has said that as a critic he is "less interested in systematic argument than in communicating the spontaneously dense, specific and often paradoxical events of consciousness in the face of contemporary works." This is a perspective that can only emerge from a deep love of art and artists. He goes further, adding: "If as a critic I remain relatively unprincipled—an amateur at heart—it's because I've learned that my pleasures come most fully from works that outstrip everyone's principles, and most especially my own—at which point everyone, even the artist, should feel amateurish, and a bit humble." Here we sense Berkson's metaphysical modesty offset by playfulness and precision (two qualities I recall him admiring in Dante and Balanchine).

When I lived in San Francisco, Berkson organized events around texts or ideas that he wanted to re-enter our conversation. One evening was dedicated to a roundtable reading of John Ashbery's epic *Europe* (1972), the first public reading in its entirety. Another was focused on W. H. Auden, and a large number of poets and artists shared work (both their own and their favorites by Auden). I read something I had written on the friendship between Auden and Hannah Arendt, citing this passage from the philosopher:

> The activity of knowing is no less a world-building activity than the building of houses. The inclination or the need to think, on the contrary, even if aroused by none of the time-honored metaphysical, unanswerable "ultimate questions," leaves nothing so tangible behind, nor can it be stilled by allegedly definite insights of "wise men." The need to think can be satisfied only through thinking, and the thoughts which I had yesterday will satisfy this need today only to the extent that I can think them anew.

This is from an essay called *Thinking and Moral Considerations,* dedicated to Auden, who she says embodied this concept of thinking as a moral good in and of itself. In a similar way Bill Berkson best represents this—his vast reading and continued curiosity rooted in a love of living itself.

Auden said that "art is divided not between the good and the bad, but between the interesting and the boring, and what is interesting is the exceptional." I believe Berkson would agree, insofar as he has written that "history is where artists and art works converse." We might more easily talk about whether any particular person's contribution to the art conversation is provocative, fresh, and delightful, or not. After all, looking is a way of thinking and is intimately tied to conversing, with artists and writers living and dead—what he was getting at in his 2008 lecture "The Divine Conversation," which begins by describing conversation as "the intense extended talk people generate among themselves, but also a kind of telepathy between the things some people do and those others who don't but find them interesting to confront and then the things that follow from that. And so on, everywhere." Berkson's dedication to dialogue as a constructive act is his closest thing to a methodology, coupled with the belief that art and criticism should open up, rather than close down, possibilities.

Bill Berkson's poetry and prose are formidable and hold an important place for the many lucky enough to know his writing, but the significance of his life in postwar American culture is something more than the sum of his published texts. Bridging several generations of New York and West Coast artists and poets of vastly diverse artistic temperament, his role of social and intellectual connector and interlocutor tends to get lost as those directly involved move onward. And so one of the purposes of this collection is to preserve evidence of these ephemeral intersections so they might be available for future artists and writers.

Three years ago now, Isabelle Sorrell and I wrote to about a hundred people, soliciting poems, essays, memoirs, and drawings for this book. The response was overwhelming, immediate, and very often to the effect of ,"For Bill: anything"—which became the title of the project. When I was an art student, it was Bill who first suggested I begin to write, and he has continued to nurture my work—the kind of gift that can never be properly repaid. I know I am not the first—and will not be the last—to benefit from this sparkling intelligence and generosity of spirit. May this book be many new friends' warm introduction to Bill Berkson, and express all our gratitude for his part of our world.

ISABELLE SORRELL

Introduction · *Poet, Art Critic, and Teacher*

POET

A good traveler is one who does not know where he is going to,
and a perfect traveler does not know where he came from.

—Lin Yutang

Although English is not my native tongue, Bill Berkson's writing—so witty,
intelligent, sonorous, and engaging—has always struck me as a kind of
laboratory of invention in that language. His poems are so open and invit-
ing that the question of passing through the thresholds of his language
is impossible to resist. His ability to play with words as though they were
made of rubber prompted me one day to ask him directly:

> How? When? Were you able to write like you do? Did something click
> one day or did it happen by increments? I know that your father was
> a journalist and those fields are cousins, so you were bathed in the
> word-world at a young age; but when did you make it yours?

He replied, "You know, I've been doing this for a long time." Needless to say,
I disbelieved him entirely and took his response as an overly humble retort.

When I met the poet Duncan McNaughton for a second time, I decided
to ask him about the inspired craftsmanship of Berkson's writing. "Berkson,"
McNaughton replied, "got that really early; it was already there in his late
teens, early twenties." Indeed, if one looks into his writing of the late '50s
and early '60s, it is clear that language is already his true friend and accom-
plice. But *how* he acquired this ability has nagged at me. In fact, it is a com-
plete enigma. Look at this fragment from his poem "Still Earth," written
in 1961:

> I'm wondering how to fill it, that sack you left me
> of sky, redundant as an egg, entering the breakfast room
> with a careless smile—

Or here:

A drip in the bucket
                    glass of Red Cheek apple juice
the mere continental drift
                    "Did
they really want to come back with us
and if so to do what do you think?
                    the responses of dawn are very gulpy
      a second deafness
says
      "There's an apple   on the table
        it's dawn   I die"
Days when the dictates of grimey angels perspire
nothing but sulk fever or
                    Tooth-on-nail
              I can't quite make it
"Who were they anyway
what did they want
and why didn't they get it?
                    A sunny world full of doodling idiots
            it's because the roof leaks
            it's because the tummy grows
                    and the crumpled daisies get thrown out—
because they showed up anyhow, those persnickety inchworms,
                    tunneling through and on
into the core where it counts but you don't pay

The title of this poem is "Enigma Variations." It is dedicated to Jim Carroll.
But *Enigma Variations* is also the title of a book Berkson did with Philip
Guston in 1975, and is the first piece of writing of his I came upon. (And
because of its mixture of freshness and intelligence, it remains one of my
favorites to this very day.) About two decades from that initial reading,
puzzled about what I (as a foreigner) could and should not be missing,
I once again wrote him:

Dear Bill,
    There is something that has been trotting intermittently in my
    head for months or probably years and while I tend to cultivate things

that are mysterious to me, today is the day that I seem to crave for an explanation.

Could you, would you tell me a little bit about "Enigma Variations"? I hope that my asking is not "vulgarité de l'esprit."

For example, on the cover of Enigma Variations, there is "that" piece from Guston, did he do the drawing first or did you respond to the drawing? what prompted you (if it was you) to choose it as the title of the book? etc.

I would really appreciate this,
Thanks, Isabelle

His reply:

Dear Isabelle,

Here it goes, swiftly, because I am preparing two classes for tomorrow.

Enigma Variations is a piece of music by the English composer Sir Edward Elgar, who is best known for *Pomp and Circumstance* (played at most English royal functions). Sir Frederick Ashton made a ballet on it for Covent Garden. I saw this performed in New York in the early 1960s.

But the poem was occasioned in 1968 by Jim Carroll's telling me he was going with Edwin Denby to the Covent Garden (or Royal) Ballet at the Met and that one of the dances that night was *Enigma Variations*. Jim was sharing my apartment on 57th Street at the time, and we were sitting in the living room, in which was also my desk.

When Jim said *Enigma Variations* I immediately started this poem—not unusual in those days—incorporating various things that were on my mind of late. "There's an apple on the table . . ." that quote comes from a big poem painting by Frank O'Hara and Norman Bluhm that hung next to the desk (I have the work here, in our bedroom). The ending derives from a funny routine Jean Shepherd did on the radio, driving up to a toll booth at the Hudson Tunnel and refusing to pay and recording the whole thing for his radio show. (Jim always thought it was a remark about how he didn't pay any share of the rent, but he was wrong, I never cared or thought about that.)

In the 1970s, Philip Guston and I talked often about doing a book together. "Enigma Variations" had already been in a small book called

Recent Visitors. The book Guston and I eventually did, in 1975, had that and poems from various years 1968–75. I always thought there was a lot of enigma in Guston's painting and my poetry, and that, as well as a mutual nod to Giorgio de Chirico, made "Enigma Variations" seem an appropriate title for the book.

Then again there is the drawing Guston did or selected (not sure which) to face that poem in the book: it is a true enigma, a living room, no people, weird big-like rug, funny no-top drapes, a chair like . . . an enigma, I guess!

Funny, I just realize that the drawing and Frank and Norman's poem painting hang on either side of Connie's and my bed.

Love, Bill

Now, when I read "Enigma Variations," my original take is no doubt altered, neither for better nor for worse, simply altered, dotted by a cornucopia of new information, new script, new characters, etc. It is thanks to the words, their relationship and positioning on the page, that the poem retains the atmosphere of that first experience—of engagement in variations. And so, the Enigma prevails!

Take note that he said "swiftly" at the outset of his response because he was preparing to teach two classes the following day. And so, as one reads the letter, two feelings occur simultaneously. There is the feeling that the explanation conveys, and the feeling of being moved by a reply of such length and thoroughness in spite of his time commitment. My experience (and I know I am not alone in this) is that he is never short, never reluctant to give. Rather, his generosity is legendary.

To cite another example—in 2004 my neighbors and I were applying for a grant to improve our run-down mini-park in San Francisco. As I come from a background in which one is not supposed to interrupt people older than oneself with unnecessary disturbances, I originally requested help from another of my writer friends. When this capable person did not respond, my last recourse was to ask Bill. Again, he was quick to reply.

Dear Isabelle,

I would be glad to look over the proposal and make editorial suggestions. Can you email it to me?

Best, Bill

This was written on June 11, 2004, when Bill had been carrying an oxygen tank twenty-four hours a day for about a year. His health by then was precarious, his life on a thread, or, more accurately, at the end of a thread. But his spirit was always bright, as if a light illuminated him from inside. He would not permit anyone to torment themselves about his health and always smiled back when the oxygen mask wasn't in his way. Months later I would hear from Connie Lewallen, his wife, that the doctor had called to say that her husband was on his last days unless a set of organs showed up. On June 18 (seven days after my request), young lungs found their way into that thoracic cage which was obviously not ready to go, as since then he has continued to dare, enchant, and enlight the world of the living.

ART CRITIC

> My task which I am trying to achieve is, by the power of the written word to make you hear, to make you feel—it is, before all, to make your self.
>
> —JOSEPH CONRAD

As an art critic, Bill Berkson's poetry feeds his love for looking at art and reporting "about seeing and what can be seen," as Frank O'Hara once put it. His descriptions are crafted from the detailed matter he finds by looking, thinking, and saying. For a visual artist like myself, looking and thinking are like oxygen to the lungs, while the effortless eloquence with which Berkson writes his essays keeps me wide awake. In brief, Berkson's dispatches as an art critic bear witness to "The Art of Now"—the title of one of his seminars at the San Francisco Art Institute in the '80s. Take for instance the sparkling insights in this review of Robert Ryman in *Artforum* (May 1988):

> . . . Ryman's five paintings aren't images. They require a minimum encounter of 30 seconds to make any kind of dent. Inspect the surface and you see a wealth of detail seemingly more unusual and quirkier than its sum; turn away (or leave the room) and you wonder if you saw anything particular at all. The aphoristic sweep makes the clearest recollection of detail seem desultory. As in William Carlos Williams' poem "The Descent": "no whiteness (lost) is so white as the memory / of whiteness."

Charter, 1985, which could be considered the prototype for the series, states a theme that the other, later pictures sift through and expand. This is an array of two white near-squares and three raw-metal rectangles done on a single, bent aluminum sheet that slips vertically along, then away from and back to the wall where the upper "square" begins and ends. It's fastened near the edges at the top, upper middle, and bottom by bolts. The protruding boltheads join in the pictorial mix by twos, dotting the corners and peeking out from the shade cast by the cantilever. The object's variegated light unfolds and regathers with an arcane orderliness like that of circular breathing in music . . .

TEACHER

> You have brains in your head.
> You have feet in your shoes.
> You can steer yourself
> Any direction you choose . . .
>
> —DR. SEUSS

Let's not forget that Bill Berkson is a teacher of art history and literature, perhaps one of the last luminaries in higher education who is able to teach without a BA in hand. To this rather unusual phenomenon, he would simply say that he was hired on merit and that, true, the days when that was able to happen have vanished. There is something incredibly inspiring about studying with an erudite individual who has bypassed the predictable array of PhDs found in academia today. This excitement is boosted by the rebellion such a choice suggests, and reflects how Berkson is always one to question the status quo, a quality one finds in the wisdom he has passed down to those of us lucky enough to have taken his classes. In fact, one can find enthusiastic reports about Berkson's teaching as far back as 1966, when he was only twenty-seven and teaching at the New School for Social Research in New York. In 1978, Frances Lefevre Waldman, who was attending Berkson's course, wrote her daughter, young poet Anne Waldman:

> Then last night B. gave a special workshop and it was terrific. I realize how much I owe him for my original education in the poetry of

Bill Berkson and Philip Guston at Gallery Paule Anglim, San Francisco, January 1979

our time and how nobody else even approaches his level. Formidable critic sense . . .

Many have felt something similar over the years. A sample of this valuable advice to students can be found in the beginning of his *For the Ordinary Artist: Short Reviews, Occasional Pieces and More*:

> In the perplex of recent human history, the certainties of today's academic ideologues look arrogant to the point of soullessness. Marxism, accurate in its structural understanding, has only a general theory of ethics. By now, the idea that art, artists, and more to the point, art students are born on the side of fair play—willfully tidy classroom Marxists all—is normal and wrong. It is important to have a firsthand, vivid sense of the issues and stakes involved in philosophical discussion, for which literacy is a good start and intelligent conversation (including talking back aggressively to what you read) an advance requirement. But the talk has to advance beyond the citation or précis of what you have read; as [Robert] Storr said, you want it brought home. What

Kant or Kristeva has written regarding this or that is no particular consequence unless you make it so; depending on what you see in what is written, what you say or do in turn is the only realization it may ever find.

In 1989, the artist Paul Kos, also teaching at SFAI, was asked about "fame" in an interview. Kos replied, "Bill Berkson said something recently that made a lot of sense, 'When you are young, you want to be a famous artist; when you are older, you want to do something that matters.'"

For Bill, ANYTHING

JOE BRAINARD   Portrait of Bill Berkson; 1971

JOHN ASHBERY

Five O'Clock Shadow

Whence I came is
"very different," looks pretty,
balkanized already.

Things bother you along.
It's so interesting when
the beautiful things on the table
listen, in a trance.

What's an afternoon among friends?
What can you do?

JOHN BALDESSARI

Bill and I go back to "in the day" when, it seems, all things were possible and all things happened. Bill was one of the newest luminous personalities I met through Frank O'Hara and the folks associated with "the New York School." We were very schooled off in those days but finally in one important goodness, to free American poetry from the "varmint" of academic bloodlessness ok I mean the "Beats," Black Mountain, San Francisco gatherers, and the New York folk, meaning O'Hara, Koch, Ashbery, and some others. And later, the Black Arts Movement. Bill came, laughing and energetic, as a welcome reinforcement in that struggle even if it was, as Ginsberg called it, "the era of good feeling."

What Bill Berkson brought was not only his "Young Tennis Pro" profile but a poetry and reasoning that was open, strong, and surprisingly wise, yet fundamentally unaffected by the virus of dullness which has lately begun to re-infect the public literary muse.

That Bill has reached that place where we must produce a festschrift for him makes me hopefully yearn for a "Sankofa" time amongst the most thoughtful of us, where we can go forward by looking backward.

But to Bill, personally, he knows we got to keep on pushin'.

ALAN BERNHEIMER

for Bill Berkson

The difference between
truth serum and asterism

The dark of the matinee
and fathomably lovely

dirigible shadow moving
at dirigible speed across

the 1920s Oakland Tribune
facade a year ago today

Apart life with caper delivery
just around the cornice

Maybe Monk in Oslo
and elevator men at this remove

TED BERRIGAN

Clown

for Bill Berkson

There's a strange lady in my front yard
A girl naked in the shower, saying
"I'm keeping my boxes dry!" A naked artist
Smoking. Bad teeth. Wooden planks: furniture. Sky
One minute ago I stopped thought: 12 years of cops
In my life. & Alice is putting her panties on
Takes off a flower dress for London's purple one
Out of the blue, a host of words, floating
March: awaiting rescue: smoke, or don't
Strapped: deprived. Shoot yourself: stay alive.
& you can't handle yourself, love, feeling
No inclination toward that solitude.
Take it easy, & as it comes. Coffee
Suss. Feel. Whine. *Shut up.* Exercise.
Turn. Turn around. Turn. *Kill dog.*
Today woke up bright & early, no mail, life
Is horrible, & I am stupid, & I think . . . Nothing.
"Have faith, old brother. You are a myth in my heart.
We are both alive. Today we may go to India."

GREGG BIGLIERI

Stems

> To Bill:
> If you know what I mean, then you know what I know.

One of the offshoots stemming from working on your talks for *Sudden Address* was the beginning of a correspondence and a sharing of lists regarding the sublime. What I like to think of as another link in the endless chain letter of the sublime: a series of decisions and excisions, precise substitutions and incisive restitutions, the modulated breathing of exact quotation. Bill's great line about the sublime from his book with Bernadette Mayer: "What otherwise can be the big draw about The Sublime other than that there are no mirrors in it?" At one point Bill said something like, "I assume you know Mandelstam's 'On the Addressee.'" And I remember having thought, "Haven't I already not read that yet?" And yet . . . Perhaps I had heard of it through Celan's "Meridian" talk. And yet how could you have known that I was in the process of reading Mandelstam's "Conversation about Dante," which contains that touchstone for me on the sublime and quotation: "A quotation is not an excerpt. A quotation is a cicada. It is part of its nature never to quiet down." Every word takes you back to the place it gives, as it takes back what it gives to you. You give a bit, buckle, and take what it has to give, what, at the secret speed of sound, sounds. "A cello delays sound, hurry how it may." When I hear you, I know you're listening.

Before I even knew Bill and yet after I had already read him. That is, read what he had been reading and thinking and writing through—as in Blake's reference to seeing through the eye of corporeal vision—"I look thro' it & not with it"—the same goes for quotations. We are able to see through them because they are not transparent. That chain letter began many years ago when my friend Adam DeGraff had passed along a homophonic translation of a passage from "El Egg" to Bill, who then created his own version at a third remove. This was the subterranean beginning of our chain letter, disguised as a game of homophonics. And translation is yet another of the sublime's allusive engines.

Reading Bill's talks without ever having met him, yet knowing him through what he read and talked about, it was such a pleasure to see connections and the new strands of thinking his writing makes possible. Reading through his talks on the work of others makes me want to write, imbibe the energy Bill brings to the task, and make my own strands. Bill's criticism is the best kind of criticism in that it pushes the conversation forward, it inspires and opens up space for thinking rather than collapsing it through a series of deadening reductions. As I read, I was "Sleeping on the Wing" with O'Hara and winging it. Time appears only to disappear on the threshold of the *Sudden Address* Conversations about Berkson. And not just "strands," as Bill used the term, but more like stems. The chain letter of the sublime is forged not by links or strings but stems, attached and unfurling, extending tentatively like fingertips addressed to other fingertips. Bit by bit, but neither bit nor bridle, these stems are more than systems; they are worlds in grains of sand, words in the grain of words. The concept doesn't trickle down to the particular; rather, the particular grain of sand is already part of the beach, it makes up the beach, it is the beach—each is a beach. The stem is an integral of the system. To cancel out the system in the process of thinking, we light from stem to the stem. "Words are budding": Stems.

So, Bill, I think you know what I mean even though I don't know what you think. We understand each other because we both don't know what to think, but we know how to think about it. We seem to know to whom we are speaking, to whom we are addressing these messages in these particular bottles. Suddenly, what we see in the addressee is the word *address* and the word *see*. What we see are the forms of address. I see through and not with you and thus see so much more than myself (no mirrors), and more than I ever thought I could see before I had the experience of seeing through your words. I was thinking about a book of dreams, but it was better far to dream of books and of the writing to come. Books are pillows for dreams, cushions between minds, spaces where two heads touch to form a new bed, not to sleep on but to read on. If address be the form of love, read on. The tide of sublime address will never be stemmed. If I know what you mean, then I know what you know. It's as if we're sleeping on bunk beds made of little books. Just because we copied each other's pillows doesn't mean we'll have the same dreams.

A balloon looks through a keyhole and then passes through it to the other side.

LIFE BEGINS AT ZERO

BY *Bill Berkson*

AND *Joe Brainard*

JOE BRAINARD

SEX IN THE MORNING LOOKS LIKE THIS.

UNLESS YOU ARE QUEER.

In which case, it isn't really <u>sex</u>.

(UNLESS YOU ARE QUEER)

That certainly is a queer thought, Joe.

WHAT THIS CARTOON NEEDS IS A PLOT.

11 P.M. The sun is out. We are inside, beating our brains out! And for what?

For you, that's what. That's what collaborating is all about. Why don't you

try it sometime, instead of sitting out there, in the sun, on your ass, listening to the birds? Don't you know those birds are queer? They just perch on their little feet and giggle at you. Do you enjoy that kind of humili-ation? Do you enjoy humiliation at all? We don't. We know better. That's why we're

HERE, YOU QUEER!

"We eat

I WOULD LIKE TO TELL YOU THE STORY OF THIS PLATE. HOWEVER, THIS PLATE HAS NO STORY.

IN FACT, IT NEVER HAS AND NEVER WILL. YOU DON'T CARE. YOU HAVE NEVER LIKED STORIES ANYWAY, HAVE YOU?

and run

THE END

33

DAVID CARRIER

"Bill and I": A Sentimental Memoir for Bill Berkson

> The love for pictures was by no means dead in Venice, and
> Longhi painted for the picture-loving Venetians their own
> lives in all their ordinary domestic and fashionable phases. . . .
> There is no tragic note anywhere. Everybody dresses, dances,
> makes bows, takes coffee, as if there were nothing else in the
> world that wanted doing.
> —BERNARD BERENSON

In fall 1999 I was a Getty scholar, in residence for the academic year in
Brentwood, trying to write a book about art museums. The project went
frustratingly slowly. The literature is vast, and soon my desk was cov-
ered with books and bad drafts of my own would-be manuscript. The
more I read, the less I knew what I wanted to say. And so in November
I took a break, flying up to San Francisco to visit Bill. I didn't go there to
do research, but went just as an art tourist. And so it happened that we
went together to the Legion of Honor. Bill and I had talked about pictures
before. In the summer of 1991, we spent some time in San Francisco's
museums, and I had the pleasure of speaking to his class at the Art Institute
there. But although I always enjoyed our conversations, it wasn't until 1999
that I was ready to learn from these shared experiences.

All significant art history originates before works of art. Where else?
People see a painting and talk about it, evolving in the company of friends
a vocabulary adequate to the occasion. When Vasari discusses Michelan-
gelo; when Bellori talks about Poussin; when Clement Greenberg praises
Jackson Pollock; when Joachim Pissarro discusses Jasper Johns and Robert
Rauschenberg: then their commentaries gain authority from these personal
relationships. Such free conversation is the necessary foundation of art
history writing. But academic writers organize and regiment these conver-
sations, organizing them into structures, which, by treating them as objec-
tively valid, destroy their lived value. Art historians critique and evaluate
Vasari's judgments about Michelangelo, Bellori's account of Poussin, and
Greenberg's descriptions of Pollock. By turning these conversations into
subjects of art historical knowledge, something is gained, for this writing
becomes the basis for intellectual discourse. But something also is lost,
which now I seek to recover, or at least to understand.

When Bill and I went to the Legion of Honor, after looking at paintings by more notable artists, it happened that we focused on two paintings by Pietro Longhi (1702–1785). Sometimes called an Italian Watteau, or linked with his contemporary, the playwright Carlo Goldoni, he is one of those many respectable old masters who do not attract much attention. Only a few do: Piero della Francesca (about whom Bill has written marvelously); Caravaggio; or, thanks to his political involvement with the end of the Old Regime, Jacques-Louis David. In Longhi's time, Venice was declining. And soon after his death, the life of the Republic, conquered by Napoleon, ended, and the city became just the center of the tourist industry now celebrated in Donna Leon's marvelous detective stories.

Longhi chronicles this fascinating period of decline, showing the social life of eighteenth-century patrician Venetians. But notwithstanding the efforts of some ingenious recent commentators to treat him as a politically critical artist or, as I noted, a great painter, the Venetian Watteau, he remains marginal. His near contemporary Giovanni Battista Tiepolo (1696–1770) is challenging because he can legitimately be understood as the last Italian master in the grand tradition inaugurated by Cimabue and Giotto. By comparison, Longhi is merely a very good genre painter, not an artist deserving of any special attention.

No doubt this is why Bill and I found the two Longhis in San Francisco such a satisfying subject for conversation. If an artist employs a challenging iconography, as Nicolas Poussin often does, then conversation is easily inhibited. Viewing a Tibetan Buddhist scroll, one might wonder what that image from an unfamiliar culture depicts. But Longhi is, by contrast, an unchallenging painter. No doubt you would need to consult a social historian to understand exactly what is going on in his scenes. We looked at two pictures, *The Music Lesson* and *The Mandolin Recital*. In both, you see a group of Venetians enjoying music. Even without knowing what this music sounds like, or the exact social status of the listeners, one can readily talk about the pictures.

In the Legion of Honor, Bill and I discussed the place of these pictures in the history of Venetian art and their relation to genre painting, offering a sketch of the implied narratives. And we made some observations that took debate into the present. We noted, for example, that Longhi's blank backgrounds anticipate those in the contemporary figurative art of Alex Katz. Art critics are very familiar with this situation, in which conversation is improvised in front of pictures. If you are writing a review, it can be immensely helpful to visit the show with a sympathetic interlocutor, someone who may see things you don't or whose presence encourages you to articulate thoughts. Having a supportive companion is especially helpful when looking at contemporary art, for then the terms of discourse are not settled. Looking at Poussin, one tries to recall (and perhaps argue with) the literature. But in a Whitney Biennial or in the Chelsea galleries, since there are no entrenched verbal assessments of the art at hand, one must extemporize. I love the challenge of doing that.

Denis Diderot, William Hazlitt, Charles Baudelaire, and a few modernists: these critics are our heroes because they are the ones whose writing matters. Art historians have a different list of heroes, for while they use critics' commentaries as essential evidence, they seek to regiment this writing. That, after all, is why art history is an academic subject and art criticism is not. We art critics are all self-taught—many, like Bill, are poets. No doubt, then, our academic colleagues think us scatterbrained, lacking in discipline. Bill offers a note-perfect characterization of our activity:

> Poets bring a technical proficiency to art writings as well as an attitude that, in art's increasingly institutional settings, seems proportionally ever more off the wall. Their interventions carry a fierce love of language and an abiding curiosity about the world of things. Perhaps more than the full-time critics, they simply want to say something interesting about the things they've seen . . .

You can read a great deal of art history without thinking that the writer wants to say something interesting.

The development of art history as an academic industry was so inevitable that complaints would be futile. One might as well complain there are no more cheap rent-controlled apartments in the East Village or dealers selling inexpensive old master prints in midtown Manhattan. The world and so also the art world have changed. This very commercial art world system needs collectors, curators, and dealers, but it's increasingly unclear what role critics have. Our marginal economic role surely reflects this situation.

Under the old regime, art and its interpretation was subject to top-down control. One reason that free discussion of art in the emerging public sphere of the museum seemed very important was that it was reasonable to hope for a cross-over into the larger public realm. Once, in the Parisian salons of the 1760s, the French talked freely about art, they were prepared to discuss politics also. But this, the ambition of the Enlightenment, is as yet unfulfilled. As has often been observed, although many contemporary artists are concerned with politics, the specialized terms in which debate is presented drastically restrict the audience. Nowadays, museums attract very large audiences, but since most contemporary art doesn't really speak to the broader public, neither does commentary on it by critics. Poetry, as Bill has observed, has even smaller audiences. But unlike writing, contemporary visual art requires expensive large public spaces.

Art critics speak, at best, to the happy few. And yet there is an obvious paradox in the way that art history has marginalized criticism. In art, what attracts attention is radical innovation. The heirs of the Abstract Expressionists were Johns, Rauschenberg, and Warhol—very different artists—whose most interesting successors, in turn, made very different works. Nothing is less interesting than merely continuing tradition. But while we seek bold originality in art, in art writing we desire academic discipline. I grant, the most interesting art historians challenge readers because they are radically original. My list of living heroes, Svetlana Alpers, T. J. Clark, Michael Fried, Rosalind Krauss, Linda Nochlin, and Leo Steinberg, might differ from yours. But we could agree, I believe, that art historians matter when they are as original as our artists. Soon enough, of course, these writers attract regularizing commentary. And then their ways of thinking become merely academic.

Nothing I have said is meant to undercut the value of conversations in front of works of art. But it does raise questions about how to place this activity. What is the function, I am asking, of such conversations? Aesthetically speaking, there is nothing I value more. "Painting must be before all things decorative," Walter Pater said: "a thing for the eye, a space of colour on the wall . . . whatever higher matter of thought, or poetry, or religious reverie might play its part therein." But in our visual culture, the aesthetic has long been beleaguered, and so some defense of this attitude is required. The goal of the art writer, as I understand our task, is to respond to painting on these, Pater's, terms.

For very many years, I have found Bill to be the most sympathetic of companions, both on those occasions when we have looked at art together and at those many times when he has generously commented on my writing in progress. I have gained much often from rereading his writings and often, I hope not to his frustration, been inspired to disagree. From Bill I have learned the importance of going my own way. Without such friendship, what value could life have? This is what I have learned from him. But I would not wish to make a friend responsible for my foolish, perhaps irresponsible claims.

Jim Carroll and Bill Berkson in Bolinas 1970; photo by Aram Saroyan

JIM CARROLL

with Bill Berkson

I walk the halls in overalls
For I am the Little King.
(1969)

TOM CLARK

In Bill's Backyard, Bolinas

Now light streams through the trees of the dream.
Dead friends idly amble through the arches
The green bower makes over our heads;
In Bill's backyard—framed for this flashback
To the days before, or perhaps during, the Flood—
Things are, as in a kind of moonlit masque
Lit up at night like the carnival scene
In *Strangers on a Train*; yet strangers
There are none, only friends; summer fog coming in
On the marine layer clockwork shuttle
Over the populous village in the dream;
Sea, hill, wood, numberless goings-on;
Off in the distance beyond Elm somewhere,
Off beyond Ocean Parkway in the mists,
A whistle buoy intermittent; blue reedy
Spiritual openness of Eric
Dolphy floating from inside the humble shack
Taking shape as words, a cool
Geometrical language; then cloudy faces
Tossed up on the cresting waves
Beyond the reef, in the dream: ghosts
Waving, not drowning. *So let's make this stroll*
Through the underworld last.

ANDREI CODRESCU

Why I Love Bill Berkson

Bill Berkson is a bird
but also a lynx and a gentleman

he was very pale and white on the beach in 1974
like a new yorker still just visiting california
but he became a dark bolinese soon after

Bill Berkson is a breathable atmosphere
around an island of delightful thoughts
a portable civilization who will read his poems
in your city if you ask or you can go to him

where he is surrounded by art and light

if I was a teacher in an art or poetry school
(once I was and I did just what I'm about to say)
I would teach berksonism as modus vivendi
a way to live poetry as art and viceversa

if I was Joe Brainard I'd write
an I Remember Bill Berkson book
because I remember Bill Berkson
from every time I saw him
and there is that book in there

which is a berksonist concept I share
namely that there are many books in there
as many as the remarkable poets one has known
and if one was suited to be the author of any of them
by either inclination or deliberation one could be that author

I know what I said
ask Bill if you think I didn't make sense
he sees sense he senses it he has an appetite for it
he is how life tastes art and poetry
he is that author and many other animals

JACK COLLUM

Bill Berkson Acrostics

Culture Lunes   <u>Little Headlines</u>

But what can
I say to Bill, besides   BASIC INK LACE
"Language loves dirt"?

Late Capitalism disgraces
Brightness by freezing it in   LIPS BETRAY ELGIN
Erasable as footage.

Recording heroics was
Karmically subject to confusion of   RHYMING KANGAROO SAUCE
Subject and object.

Only closed-eye vision
Needs to dance with focus   ONAGER NEGATES BRIGADOON
But not collapse.

Illness is interesting.
Love is less interesting but   I LOVE LOUIE
Lavishes interest about.

Bill, think you
Exaltation of suffering best, or   BEACH EDGE REMINISCENCES
Refutation of suffering?

Kissing depends on
Syncopation of two or more   KILL SEVENTY-THREE ORANGEMEN?
Opposing electrical fields

Nobody should ever
Bend light unless they're truly   NATIONAL BURNED IGLOO
Incandescent as Hell.

Lethargy leads to
Lightening being painfully internalized by   LOOKS LIKE BREAKFAST
Body or soul.

Enlightenment? Only if
Rotation & Chaos wrestle it,   ENTRANCE-LEVEL ROYAL KUDZU
Kind of irregularly.

Smoothness certainly occurs
On occasions whereon (wherein?) almost   SOMNOLENT OCHRE NECKTIES
No one's noticing.

Beauty and the
Infant—hmm, how do you   BLASPHEMY INCLUDES LOVE
Like that binary?

Literature plus music
Become(s) veritable human-cum-angel mirth, but   LUMINA BRIDGE EXTRACT
Especially on Earth.

Ripping up all
Knowledge will increase it a
Second or two.

REMARKS KINDLING SORCERY

Oh
No!

OR NOT

BILL CORBETT

Bill Berkson at CUE and Two Snapshots

Because I want to direct my attention elsewhere, I will be brief about Bill's poetry and art writing. I admire and enjoy Bill's poems. From "Stanky"—great title—through "An Ives" and to "Gloria," Bill is often unbeatable in ten lines and less. My one druther about his poetry is a wish that he write more documentary poems, like "Red Devil," "Roy Eldridge, Little Jazz," and "Signature Song." When working with facts, Bill excels.

His art writing ranks with the best written by a poet or journalist of his generation. Bill's a fine phrasemaker, and he must have notebooks full of memorable quotes. But what sets Bill apart is that he is a first-rate reporter. He has opinions, but they never overwhelm his duty, as he sees it, to inform the reader about the art he has seen. You always learn from a Berkson review, essay, or lecture.

My subject is working with Bill. When Manhattan's CUE Art Foundation opened in 2003, the painter Gregory Amenoff, one of CUE's founders, nominated Bill to curate a first show. Bill chose the painter George Schneeman. Over the years Bill developed a close relationship with CUE, on whose advisory board I sit. When asked to serve on this board, Bill said yes. We had been friends for over twenty years, but I had never worked with Bill beyond setting up a reading or talk.

When Bill arrived for CUE's twice-yearly meetings, he always came with more names of potential curators than any other board member. If he had a question, he asked it and listened intently to the answer. Professional? To a T! Bill offered up only what he knew from firsthand experience—nothing institutional or careerist about his approach. He surely knew more gossip than he let on, but this was business, and his pleasure was to get it right.

We usually finished in two hours. Bill gave us all his great smile, handshakes or hugs; then he was off to lunch or a show he had to see. Memorable to have worked with so unassuming a man entirely focused on the task at hand. Bill's character shone.

As I wrote the above, two snapshots of Bill insisted themselves:

Twenty or more years ago, John Wieners read at Harvard's Woodberry Poetry Room. John began, after complaining that he was tired of them, with a few *Hotel Wentley Poems*. Then John held up a copy of Bill's book *Lush Life*, from whose cover Bill grins. John had cut through the book to the spine twice, making a flipbook that allowed him to combine different pages. Before he read these exquisite corpse poems, John held up the book's cover again and said, "Not just another pretty face."

Bill and I had a drink at Jeremiah Tower's restaurant STARS in San Francisco. It must have been in the 1980s—we were just getting to know each other. I remember that the bartender had been a student of Bill's but can recall nothing of our conversation. As we left, Bill pointed to his green mud-spattered car parked akimbo outside the posh restaurant. The car's hood had muddy hoofprints across it left by some animal that morning in Bolinas, where Bill then lived. "A deer," Bill laughed. "They do it all the time."

Friendships between writers can take place entirely in print. I've never met Bill Berkson face to face. We've occasionally exchanged mail over some years (though not, I'm pretty sure, emails). I know him almost entirely through his work: first through his poetry, which I found as a student in the 1960s, then through his editing, with Joe LeSueur, of an unforgettable book-length homage to Frank O'Hara. But, being an art critic myself, it's primarily to his writing on art that I've been drawn. More than drawn to. There were stretches in the 1980s and 1990s when I felt I was taking a Berkson correspondence course on the fine art of art writing every time I read him in *Art in America*.

Through those articles, we spent time together and shared shaping experiences, the way friends do. With him leading the way, we took a long, enthralled walk through a museum exhibition of grand late de Kooning painting when that work was still fresh from the studio. We spent ruminative time savoring Albert York's silvery pastorals. The Berkson view of Hans Hofmann was a convincer for me on the merits of that hard-to-argue-for artist. Berkson on Franz Kline has kept that soulful sweetheart of a painter very alive in my mind.

And then there were his invaluable introductions to artists I hadn't fully noticed, many of them West Coast modernists: David Park, David Ireland, Wayne Thiebaud. "Thiebaud's Vanities" in *Art in America* in 1985 is, phrase by phrase, art writing at its very best, Marianne Moore poetry in prose:

> Northern light is nice but difficult, and not always clear. It is anything but "relentless." It lopes, jounces, jags, spreads (at its brightest like aluminum foil), and is often befogged when not rained out.
> "The flowers have fallen, the fruits have all been torn down."
> In the world of things, isn't scattered synonymous with structure?
> If things do possess us, what do they require? Just breathing space, perhaps, or, as Thiebaud has suggested, "an independent repose."

As is true with most art writing worth revisiting, thumbs-up/thumbs-down is beside the point. As a newspaper journalist for a couple of decades now, I've always felt that, above and beyond all else, what I owe my readers is a reading experience. Berkson on Thiebaud is precisely that. So is his extraordinary essay on Piero della Francesca, which appeared in *Art in America* in 1993 (where, let me add, we shared the good fortune of working with that magazine's matchless editor, Elizabeth Baker).

"What Piero Knew" is more than a museum visit. It's a Grand Tour through Tuscany and central Italy in search of the work of an elusive Renaissance master. Thousands of people have undertaken this pilgrimage over the years. I did in the late 1980s. Then the Berkson account appeared. Did I want to make the trip again, in print, with him? Are you kidding? I was thrilled.

And so we set off, going first to Arezzo to see the *Legend of the True Cross* frescoes; then to Piero's hometown, Borgo Sansepolcro, where his *Resurrection* is kept; from there to nearby Monterchi and the *Madonna del Parto* (housed in a cemetery chapel on my 1980s visit, in a museum in the 1990s); and finally to Urbino, where we linger over the inscrutable *Flagellation*.

And here is Bill Berkson talking all the way, about Piero's virtually fact-less biography, and about his shifting afterlife in art history: first buried as if in an unmarked grave, then uncovered, now transfigured, not as progenitor or concluding synthesizer but as a kind of over-there solitary, painting away in his own room, with his own thoughts and one bright lamp, the light from which has, in recent centuries, attracted other solitaries—Cézanne was one; Morandi another—not to mention hordes of devotees like me.

And on the Berkson tour we have particularly privileged access to this Piero, as he was and as he survives in history, not just through stimulating speculations about his ideas, his thinking, but through being pulled right up close to "a huge Pierian inventory of cracklings and abrasions, cracked boards and worm-hole hollowings; scalings off, oxidizings (greens gone to brown or black)."

If Piero "brings us to the particular beauties of the fresco medium," Bill Berkson brings to us the particular beauties of writing about art in both a wide and focused view; from a historical and personal perspective. We find no forced conclusions; no flaneurial snarkiness; no please-look-at-me. We get generous adult ideas delivered by an ego willing to receive and transmit, rather than grab and impose, expressed in word-perfect language poised between journalism, belle-lettrism, and something else. That being, what? Well, poetry. Personally, I've received all of this long-distance, gratefully and familiarly, like letters sent from a valued teacher and from an old friend I've yet to meet.

RICHARD DEMING

Portrait of the Artist as a Man of Letters:
Bill Berkson and the Mutuality of the Arts

Given Bill Berkson's intellect, his erudition, and the fact that he crosses the boundary between poetry and criticism so frequently, he is what one would call a "man of letters." That is a phrase that might these days sound broadly flattering, but what motivates my interest in using the phrase is the hope of framings Berkson's dual life as a poet and an art critic in such a way that we think of his body of work as more than two intertwined modes. One could settle for the standard hyphenating of labor—poet-critic—to indicate (while also segregating) his twin identities; yet that suggests a kind of alternating current as a way of thinking of Berkson's productivity. While "man of letters" might court a patina of pretentiousness, it might—if taken seriously—give a way of thinking of Berkson's criticism and his poetry as not only integrated but as a means of integration. With this in mind, we can see how Berkson's work becomes an interface of the arts—visual and lexical—that brings the eye and the voice into a kind of shared acknowledgment of the complexities of experience from which we might learn how to see the world better: "One has to envision language or it's no hope," he writes in the poem "An Example, Worthwhile" (*Portrait and Dream* 244). To which might be added the claim that one needs to give vision a language in order for us to know it as hope.

Deep within "Poet and Painter Coda," an essay that provides an occasion for him not only to sketch out the persistently collaborative nature of the art world of the 1950s but also to give the context for his poetics, Berkson writes:

> The arts establish relations among themselves by esthetic stance and
> commonality of reference. Underlying the more or less technical
> activities peculiar to any single art—words on paper, paint on can-
> vas—there is a turn of mind (expressive of what [Wallace] Stevens
> called "a universal poetry") which by attitude, stance, or world view
> becomes conversational; it's the pivot by which artists of various
> stripes talk to one another.   (*For the Ordinary Artist* 201)

Within this passage, one hears a clever pun in that the etymology of *con-versation* is *to turn about*. So a "conversation" is literally a "pivot" around which the mind turns. Such a deft pun (itself a trope, and *trope* is a word whose history also traces to *turn*) reveals Berkson's sense of the texture of words while it also illustrates that he himself is a thinker positioned at that place where the arts come into contact. Berkson is a bridge not merely in terms of his subject matter or area of inquiry but in how he thinks about the very possibilities of expression, whatever form he uses to manifest those possibilities.

In one way of thinking about criticism, we could say that it offers a textual side of a conversation with a visual artifact. A work of art is not mute except in the most literal terms, but it is a kind of material and aesthetic response to the world that does not speak its terms, it embodies them. The critic then works out that response, coaxes a version of it into language. By doing so, the critic articulates the commonality of reference. That the critic has something to say shows how at some level he or she can recognize the stance of the artwork enough to engage it and try to voice the experience that flows from that opportunity by which elective affinities make themselves known. We might call this a mutuality.

But what if the critic is also a poet? Is there some new complexity added to the mutuality? Of course, at a certain level, criticism and poetry are very different modes. One, we might say, makes insight explicit; the other—like all arts—makes insight experiential. Now, it would be easy enough to keep these two aspects separate, and perhaps it is too much to make one mode somehow accountable to the other. Yet to think of Berkson as a man of letters is to see that the critical and the poetic are varying but not discontinuous aspects of a general form of inquiry—a kind of conversation of the self, by which the mind turns toward possibilities of response and what response asks of us.

Let me return for a moment to that first sentence in the passage I just cited. Berkson insists that the arts establish relations among themselves "by esthetic stance and commonality of reference." I do not think that we are to take this as presupposing that the shared stance is an agreement on particular judgments. Indeed, that commonality is not an agreement in opinions—whether Ingres is better than Rothko, say—but in the form of life that an artist lives.[1] This "form of life" isn't biological, of course; instead,

1. Of course, the choice between Ingres and Rothko might also indicate a more profound schism between two people if the choice is motivated by a difference in the understanding of what constitutes art or what can count as art.

this refers to the collective beliefs, practices, and values that form and are formed by an understanding of the world. It is what we might describe as a way of experiencing life. In the case of any artist, the form that life takes is primarily aesthetic. Need it be said that not everyone has this form of life? Thus, Berkson's criticism reflects the fact that as a poet he is sensitive to the underlying aesthetics of language in terms of form. For a poet, language is always drawing attention to form, and an art critic brings the form of an artwork into language. We wouldn't go so far as to say that Berkson's criticism is poetry, but at a certain level his criticism speaks to the aesthetic stance and commonality of reference between his poetry and the art that he writes about in that both fix upon form. To think of one mode is to have in mind the influence of the other mode because both stand as shades of the same sustained attention. "In a hurry always, utterly remote / You insist or stumble into interest," he writes in "Serenade" (*Portrait and Dream* 182). Acts of attention are akin to moments of grace that we stumble into if we have worked to make the conditions of interest possible.

The commonality of references that provide the shape to Berkson's thinking in its various forms can be traced back to New York City, one of the most cosmopolitan of cities, where lines of thought and forms of life are constantly intermingled and intermingling. To know either Berkson's poetry or his criticism is to be aware of Berkson's relationship to the New York School of poetry, whose major figures—Frank O'Hara, Barbara Guest, Kenneth Koch, James Schuyler, and John Ashbery—all wrote art criticism as well as poems. We might even also add Fairfield Porter to the list; although of course his reputation lies in his prodigious gifts as a painter, Porter was also an impressive critic and frequently wrote for *ARTnews*, where Ashbery was editor for a time. In fact, Berkson himself worked as "a sort of glorified copy boy" at that magazine beginning in 1960, which, helmed by Thomas B. Hess in the 1950s and '60s, became the preeminent forum for the dissemination of the New York School of painting (*Sweet Singer of Modernism* 259). Berkson's time at the magazine (he would leave for Europe in 1963) served as a kind of advanced course into the ideas, arts, and aesthetics of New York during one of the most explosive eras for creativity the city has ever known, but whatever he learned on the job ratified what he was learning in the bars and parties and galleries. Irving Sandler describes the critical mass of interconnected sensibilities in the 1950s art world as arising out of a collective need for assurance. "Most important was the need to exchange ideas, to defend and promote one's aesthetic premises—and one's existential stake in them—for 'confession,' that is, the revelation of one's inmost feelings and ideas, was the verbal style" (29). Thus, the social formations developed around the need for conversation—the need to be recognized not as a celebrity or "important" (that would come in the next decade) but as a legitimate artist. Because the past and its tradition could no longer provide the necessary authorization, the artists and writers of the contemporary would serve to underwrite the value of the activity. This was the milieu that Berkson stepped into when he came back to New York—a community whose coherence came from work and conversation.

In 1959, Berkson had returned to his native New York after leaving Brown University and made his way into a class at the New School for Social Research taught by Kenneth Koch, one of the central luminaries of that first generation of the New York School of poets. Koch would introduce Berkson to countless personalities, and even on his own Berkson soon found himself in dialogue with Larry Rivers, Nell Blaine, James Schuyler, Jane Freilicher, and other bright lights of the New York scene. Though most important for Berkson among these names was Frank O'Hara—the insider's insider—whose influence on and friendship with Berkson cannot be overestimated. During that time, the city was an open constellation of intensities, and, pulled into O'Hara's gravity, Berkson learned to navigate his way through the eddying waves of influence and exposure that constituted the art world of the time. Berkson soon came to be part of what might be considered the second generation of the New York School, which included David Shapiro, Tony Towle, Joe Brainard, Ron Padgett, and numerous others. The Tibor de Nagy Gallery published his first book, giving his work the ultimate imprimatur. That gallery was the center of the specific circle of elective affinities among the poets and painters who were defining the art world in the wake of the generation of giants that included Jackson Pollock, Willem de Kooning, Mark Rothko. After that, Berkson was, as they say, a "made man."

It isn't my aim to historicize Berkson, though I do want to suggest that his cross-disciplinary tendencies were galvanized by the deep need for conversation that shaped the world within which he has circulated for more than fifty years. In 1959, Schuyler summed up the reason that the New York poets' fate was so tied to painting: "Artists of any genre are of course drawn to the dominant art movement in the place where they live: in New York it is painting" (1). But the interest was more than passing. He explained: "Kenneth Koch writes about Jane Freilicher and her paintings, Barbara Guest is a *collagisté* and exhibits; Frank O'Hara decided to be an artist when he saw Assyrian sculpture in Boston; John Ashbery sometimes tried to emulate Leger, and so on." These forebears offer models and at one time even actual mentorship for the deep interface of the arts (I almost want to call it an *interfaith*) that Berkson has learned from and continues to exemplify in various capacities throughout his own career. As Schuyler concludes in his essay, "Of course the father of poetry is poetry, and everybody goes to concerts when there are any: but if you try to derive a strictly literary ancestry for New York poetry, the main connection gets missed" (2). This genealogy assembled from across the arts that Schuyler describes traces the energy of mutuality—the arts simultaneously fueling one another—that is as true of Berkson's aesthetics as it was of that generation just ahead of him.

If we consider Berkson's two modes separately, his practice in both cuts against any notions of purity, his texts constantly marking the permeability of discursive boundaries. In his poems, Berkson consistently disrupts any solemnity by means of humor, a characteristic move of both the first and second generations of the New York School. Or a certain and surprising gravity inflects a poem that had begun with a kind of insouciant wit. Consider "After 99 Comes 100." If Berkson has a "typical" movement, it is the one we see in this poem. "After 99 Comes 100" offers a series of surprising reversals of expectations created by way of tone, all of which belie (or foreground, depending on one's own worldview) a profound sense of irony. Consider the first stanza:

> Coffee's bad for tai chi chuan
> In Southampton we had a smoke alarm
> California deems it plausible
> To trade grammar for roof tar
> The grand rondo for twilight and fog   (*Portrait and Dream* 148)

The first line, replete with staccato syllables, is, as the saying goes, funny because it's true. Then the poem moves associatively through the following lines, which seems contrary to the sequential imperative of the title. So the poem accrues its energy, arriving at a surprising final stanza:

But I want to live in this world
So long as it is just the one
Draped like mounds over an audible rest
That didn't get smashed in the process
When fate was looking

The desire the poem expresses is a complex one—to live in a world, as
long as it is only the one, the one that exists as "mounds" which begin to
sound like a funereal cairn. And is fate what kept the mounds from being
smashed, or is it that the mounds were inadvertently overlooked by fate
(the latter reading, in its implication that fate can make mistakes, develops
a form of metaphysical irony, perhaps)? Also, are the last three lines meant
to specify which world the poet is referring to? Or are they a kind of appos-
itive that describes the only world there is? There is a useful ambiguity to
the poem, but any choice that the reader makes will also reflect the agency
that the speaker describes in his choosing his world, a fact made relevant
in immediate and practical terms earlier in the poem when it is noted that
its occasion is "election day." Even if there is "just the one," the speaker still
chooses it. We might see this as being a general comment on how art in all
of its forms works—it presents the possibilities of various worlds, and gal-
leries, studios, museums, books, and readings are where these worlds flow
to the foreground and we confront which ones we recognize either in their
hope, despair, or in the fraught blessing of the everyday. On one hand, we
could think of the art critic then as a Virgil who guides and reveals what
constitutes these possible worlds and their implications. But such a trope
would assume that the art writer isn't also a bit lost. It is better to think of
the act of writing as Ariadne's thread, leading the writer and the reader
through the labyrinth of expression and its recalcitrant meaningfulness.
That is to say, artists, poets, and art writers all work to keep the terms fluid
and flexible as such means and methods coalesce into new ways of think-
ing, speaking, and feeling. How does one know the new? You recognize it.

Ralph Waldo Emerson writes in his seminal essay "The Poet," "But the
quality of the imagination is to flow, and not to freeze" (20). With this as
a guide, we can think of Berkson's subject as consistently being the imag-
ination, in any of its diverse manifestations, throughout whatever he is
writing, insofar as acts of the imagination make conversation necessary.
If there were no ambiguity, no wonder, we would have nothing to say to

one another. In the poem "Enough Already," Berkson writes, "Start a verb through the motions / All the motions ring true" (*Portrait and Dream* 234). If the world is always asking of us a response in its varying, contesting complexities, art is a response that keeps the imagination an active proposition of activity, unfolding, ringing through all the possible motions of thought and talk.

In his masterful "Divine Conversation," a lecture initially given at the School of Visual Arts in New York, Berkson returns to the trope of conversation and what it does for how we think of art's relationship to truth. "Truth is not a resemblance," he remarks, "but a gist markedly in accord with fact and feeling, literally a true-ing up with the world as you find it, with all the attendant instabilities every which way. It's in those terms, truth defined as hitting on an indeterminate eventuality, that what an artist makes can be said to be a 'real right thing'" (*For the Ordinary Artist* 20). The instabilities are not to be overcome and resolved, just as the insoluble mysteries and frustrations of daily life are not to be denied or ignored. Instead, the instabilities need to be confronted and tried out because these gaps are where the talk—the necessary conversation—begins and carries out the motions of an indeterminate eventuality, motions that continue resonating in the mind of any audience willing to step forward and listen, and look, and think, and speak. Even art criticism needs a ring of truth if we are to find its insights a usable wisdom. Berkson is thus in all his efforts the model of the man of letters as a thinker who immerses himself again and again in the instabilities and gaps between thought and expression to fashion a deeply felt, hard-won mutuality among the arts. After all, if the arts can be part of an ongoing conversation, there remains hope that we too can one day turn, face one another, and then listen.

WORKS CITED

Berkson, Bill. *For the Ordinary Artist: Short Reviews, Occasional Pieces & More.* Buffalo, NY: BlazeVox, 2010.

———. *Portrait and Dream: New and Selected Poems.* Minneapolis: Coffee House Press, 2009.

———. *The Sweet Singer of Modernism & Other Art Writings, 1985–2003.* Jamestown, RI: Qua, 2004.

Emerson, Ralph Waldo. "The Poet." *Essays: Second Series.* Cambridge, MA: Belknap Press, 1983.

Sandler, Irving. *The New York School.* New York: Harper & Rowe, 1978.

Schuyler, James. "Poet and Painter Overture." *Selected Art Writings.* Ed. Simon Pettet. Santa Rosa, CA: Black Sparrow, 1998.

STEVE DICKISON

"My Pleasure"

1. I believe Bill sleeps
   this creed is grounded in the syllogism
   all persons sleep and Berkson being a person
   more than it is in the evident matter

2. born on a Wednesday
   in the universe, into the populous world
   he leapt, all mothers weep and fathers also
   pierced by the unpresupposable cry out

3. his day August 30
   1939 has to be shared, as if a scene
   spliced into ZERO FOR CONDUCT, with 16,000
   Paris schoolchildren trundled from the city

4. enter little BB
   in a prospect of towering surface-scape
   the eyes' own face vibrating under air's touch
   what soaks in the optically mixed *vernissage*

5. the evident matter
   is replete, the expanded events phone in
   unruffled as days dissolved in a solution
   of wind and rain, cranked up reverb and echo

6. "Dante is writing
   from life…" "This is good news" even if it's foggy
   indoors, world's weather as one's respiration
   you get up, you get down, you get on with it

7. the evident matter
   comes written all over the surface of the sky
   as long as one gazes into the crystal dish
   the person in the poem can see for miles

8. the new blue studies
   will be throwing down at Market and Grand View
   like today's window whitening at its edges
   where the cloud fringes blur into plum blossom

9. "This drawing has all
   the doubting kind of energy I admired
   from the start . . . the clean exposure of feeling
   that unsure, of willing it not to be knee-jerk

10. or banal, short circuit-
    ing that, but being able to trace the dis-
    covery of feeling, moving every
    necessary way with it." (Travels With Guston)

11. "The Ordinary Art-
    ist is the one who just does the job. No sweat.
    The Ordinary Artist does whatever comes
    to hand along with an everyday will to art."

12. "... at rest (albeit
    absolutely attuned to the occasion)
    on a desert slope, beyond the rim of which
    can be glimpsed the upper portions of pyramids

    and the head of the Great Sphinx." (Music Pictures)

WORKS CITED

Berkson, Bill. *For the Ordinary Artist: Short Reviews, Occasional Pieces & More*. Buffalo, NY: BlazeVox, 2010.

———. *Sudden Address: Selected Lectures, 1981–2006*. [Brooklyn, NY]: Cuneiform, 2007.

———. *The Sweet Singer of Modernism & Other Art Writings, 1985–2003*. Jamestown, RI: Qua, 2004.

TERENCE DIGGORY

History and Childhood

Frank O'Hara's poem "For the Chinese New Year & for Bill Berkson" closes
with an emphatic denial:

> no there is no precedent of history no history nobody came before
> nobody will ever come before and nobody ever was that man
> (O'Hara 393)

Freedom from history is part of the legacy that O'Hara left to poets like
Berkson, sometimes classified as the "second generation" of the New York
School—ironically, since that label implies that somebody "came before."
But Berkson has given the topic of history a personal stamp that preserves
the individuality of his work, a value that O'Hara's lines clearly endorse. In
particular, Berkson places history in a distinctive relation to the vision of
childhood, one of the themes that mark the inheritance of the "first genera-
tion" New York School poets from the romantic tradition. "Then I became
a child again," O'Hara declares at the opening of "For the Chinese New
Year & for Bill Berkson" (O'Hara 289).

The complexity of the relation between history and childhood in
Berkson's work is compounded by the fact that each term carries both a
good and a bad sense. History in the good sense is a mode of empiricism,
"judicious study of / discernible reality" (*Portrait and Dream* 277), as a
Bush advisor puts it in "Exhibit A" (titled "The Way We Live Now" in
Our Friends Will Pass Among You Silently). The poem's irony turns on the
advisor's rejection of this definition in favor of history as a dramatic script
written and performed by those in power. "We're history's actors," the advi-
sor boasts (*Portrait and Dream* 278). This is history in the bad sense. It is
also childish in the bad sense of narcissism. "You think the world / revolves
around you" is the objection posed at the outset of "From a Childhood
#101" (*Portrait and Dream* 164). In contrast, childhood in the good sense
is another mode of empiricism, direct perception of the world apart from
imposed scripts. However, this sense of childhood, a founding principle
of romanticism, has its own bad sense that Berkson rejects: the sense of a
lost vision that cannot be recaptured or a regressive vision that denies adult

knowledge. Berkson favors "the idea of a grown-up art" (*Sudden Address* 46).

In Berkson's lecture "History and Truth," truth comes "out of the mouths of babes" to awaken perception from ideological slumber. Here, history in the bad sense is the idea of logical relationship imposed on a series of facts that may, in fact, be unrelated. The first "babe" that Berkson cites is his own daughter Siobhan, a grown-up in terms of years—in her mid-twenties at the time of the anecdote—but still an innocent with respect to the historical narrative imposed on paintings in the Museum of Modern Art, where she found herself "non-plussed" by a work of Picasso, as Berkson tells it (*Sudden Address* 61). To a friend's (or her father's?) explanation of the theory of Analytical Cubism, she responded simply, "Bad idea." The chaos that she actually saw in the painting came closer to the truth, Berkson implies, than the theory that attempted to make sense of what she saw. A second example features an actual "babe," Rudy Burckhardt's son Jacob at the age of two, who expressed his delight at seeing Botticelli's Venus in the Uffizi after passing through several galleries packed with Madonnas: "Nice clean lady—no baby!" (*Sudden Address* 61). In the child's view, the lady is "clean" in her separateness—standing apart not only from a baby but also from a series of other ladies.

These examples clearly reflect on the special field of history known as art history, as dictated by the occasion of Berkson's lecture, a commencement ceremony for the History of Art department of the University of California at Berkeley. The occasion allowed Berkson to define *history* in the good sense as an accumulation of facts, "knowing everything about a work of art even if all of the big original ideas about it get shredded in the process" (*Sudden Address* 62). However, since he addressed the Berkeley art historians less than a year after the traumatic events of September 11, 2001, a sense of world history, with an emphasis on politics, still hung over the event like a dark cloud. In recognition of that fact, Berkson closed his lecture by reading his prose poem "Gloria" as an example of "the subtler aspects of . . . historical reality" embodied in works of art (*Sudden Address* 62). The poem starts off with a simple emblem, an American flag, displayed ubiquitously in the months following 9/11. But the event it describes is the speaker's mishearing the sound of the flapping flag as "some poor thug running through the late September night, sneakers smacking." Like the "babes" in Berkson's previous examples, the speaker in the poem perceives a physical fact, in this case a sound, rather than the idea intended by the display of the flag. The naïve perspective of the child is also what Berkson calls, with respect to the "stance" of "Gloria," "anti- or meta-ideological."

Despite the similarities, the stance in "Gloria" is not identical to that of a child. Rather, it is the stance taken by Berkson himself in his lecture—and it makes sense to identify the "I" in "Gloria" as Berkson; New Critical distance seems pointless in this case. Just as Berkson knows that the figure in Botticelli's painting "is" Venus but recognizes, also, the truth of the child's pronouncement, "nice clean lady," so too he knows that a flag is fluttering "from the topmost balcony across the way" but nevertheless feels energized by the vision of the "poor thug" conjured up by his imagination. Berkson maintains a distinctive balance between an adult's knowledge and a child's perception. Unlike his mentor Kenneth Koch, he does not presume to speak with a child's breathless enthusiasm ("I am the horse, alive and everything"; Koch 89). The child's perceptual energy remains fully available to the adult in Berkson. He therefore avoids the elegiac tone that mourns a childhood always already lost, such as we find in O'Hara ("There I could never be a boy"; O'Hara 216). Among his predecessors in the "first-generation" New York School, James Schuyler may offer the closest analogue to the innocent yet adult perspective that Berkson adopts in his poems. It is not surprising to find Schuyler's poem "Hudson Ferry" quoted at the outset of Berkson's lecture on "History and Truth": "You can't get at a sunset naming colors" (*Sudden Address* 57). But while Schuyler proceeds from this insight toward a phenomenology (the sunset), Berkson heads toward nominalism (the problem of naming).

"Start Over," a long prose poem sequence of 1979–80, explores the problem of naming as it plays out between the perspectives of adult and child, represented by Berkson and his son Moses, of nursery-school age. This contrast of viewpoints explicitly aligns the adult with "history" and the child with "prehistory": "Thus does prehistory enter your life" (*Portrait and Dream* 198). (The significance of this statement to Berkson is indicated by the fact that he repeats it in another poem, "No Claim to the Puzzle" [*Portrait and Dream* 217].) History enters as an attempt to order the life, to compose biography. Berkson says of his relation to his son: "I am his Boswell as parenthood furthers constant biographical notice and the distinctions come more various and pronounceable than between personality-bearing and history-starved adults" (*Portrait and Dream* 190).

The question of what is "pronounceable" arises from Moses's game of assigning "various" names to the days of the week, as described in the sentences immediately preceding: "Mose pronounces a different name-day for every day of the week. Today being Sunday he pronounces Saturday and later amends that to Monday." The arbitrary nature of naming, which the child understands intuitively, threatens the adult's sense of reality, which depends on the assumption that the ideas in his mind, represented by names, correspond to real things outside his mind. The defeat of that assumption would lead to the "pointless feel of looking on without words," as Berkson describes it in "Start Over" (*Portrait and Dream* 197). In his later lecture on "History and Truth," however, he emphasizes the truth of such pointlessness: "Some facts, I believe, exhibit their true colors best by remaining beautifully, resolutely pointless. Authoritative history, however, has no appetite for pointless stories" (*Sudden Address* 59). The "pointless feel" is thus also the sense of prehistory identified with the child in "Start Over." Experienced "without words," it is also preverbal. In "Start Over," Berkson calls it "non-verbal" (*Portrait and Dream* 187), an experience he at first denies but ultimately reaffirms under the romantic label of the "ineffable": "Lift eyes to trees, tops, walking, an obviously scary bliss. Light colors of roses on a bush, paper trash in someone's front yard. A beaut'. Ineffable's the base" (*Portrait and Dream* 197). Appropriately, he segues immediately to a recollection of such experience "when a kid."

In general, Berkson's poetry does not draw very frequently on memories of his own childhood. "I'm not very conscious of my childhood," he told Bernadette Mayer (*What's Your Idea* 18). However, it seems likely that the consciousness he denies has to do with childhood's role in the story of a life, in biography, rather than the sensations a child actually experiences. In a 1984 talk at the Poetry Project, Berkson expressed frustration with the childhood section of artists' biographies as merely a "delay": "either fraught with phantoms, deprived, or idyllic" (*Sudden Address* 38). The "idyllic" account, of course, is the one that made the child a hero of romantic poetry, and it is therefore especially liable to meet resistance in a post-romantic, even postmodern poet like Berkson. In his correspondence with Mayer, he offers one childhood recollection that exhibits this resistance at the same time that it affirms sensation, in contrast to story, as a viable mode of memory: "I used to trap bees in a kind of lilac flower by the house & every so often get stung for my sadism. I also used to get

65

stung & bit a lot around the eyes by bee, wasp, spider, etc. Endless summer days of puffed-up one eye or another, & Epsom salts" (*What's Your Idea* 133). Epigrammatic rather than epic in form, the content of this little anecdote turns Wordsworth on his head: it is anti-moralistic (we do not really believe that nature is punishing the young Berkson for his "sadism") and anti-mythic (dissolving the childhood idyll of "endless summer days" in a bath of Epsom salts).

Just as the naïveté of the child can expose the fiction of historical narrative, history as fact—history in the good sense—can correct the romantic idealism associated with the child by opposing a kind of materialism. "History itches," Berkson writes in one of his earliest poems, entitled "History" (*Portrait and Dream* 34). The sensation is similar to those bee stings and bug bites recalled in his letter to Bernadette Mayer, and indeed, in "History" there are hints that Berkson is "remembering Belle Terre" (*Portrait and Dream* 37), the exclusive community on the North Shore of Long Island where Berkson spent his childhood summers. If the name Belle Terre carries idyllic associations, so does the most explicit reference to children contained in "History," in a passage that grows directly out of the statement "History itches":

> and someone opens the car door right onto a beach
>   and says, "This is your Cythera, have a run,"
>   and children jump from your back
>   unhurt, into the sand which divides them from you
>
>   (*Portrait and Dream* 35)

Here, the name of the idyllic locale is Cythera, the island of love, but, especially in the famous painting by Watteau, a love idealized as innocent and even childlike (putti abound in Watteau's painting, particularly in the Berlin version). In the poetic tradition, however, an even stronger association connects Berkson's lines with the famous image of children "sporting" on the beach in Wordsworth's "Immortality" ode:

> Hence in a season of calm weather
>   Though inland far we be,
> Our Souls have sight of that immortal sea
>   Which brought us hither,

Can in a moment travel thither,
And see the Children sport upon the shore,
And hear the mighty waters rolling evermore.   (Wordsworth 190)

The speed with which the imagination transports the viewer to this child-hood idyll is common to Wordsworth and Berkson, though Berkson updates the technology through his reference to a car. A significant differ-ence between Wordsworth and Berkson lies in the ability to overcome the distance between the adult point of view and that of the sporting children. Wordsworth simply erases the distance; "Though inland far we be," we can nevertheless see the children on the shore. Berkson's "you," though placed at the shore with the children, nevertheless confronts "the sand which divides them from you." An idealized return to childhood is prevented by sand, something that itches, like history.

For most readers of Berkson, Wordsworth would not be the first poet to come to mind for purposes of comparison, even to emphasize contrast, as I intend. Nevertheless, there is evidence that Berkson has kept Wordsworth in mind throughout his career. In "Start Over," he vulgarizes the opening line of Wordsworth's famous sonnet with the insertion of one word, "The world is too much fucking with us" (*Portrait and Dream* 192). The under-lying sentiment seems to be one that Berkson is willing to endorse, but he does not endorse the corollary belief that our own powers diminish in direct proportion to the increase of the world's powers. This is the prob-lem for which Wordsworth seeks a solution in the return to childhood, the period of life before we become alienated from that chief power of our being, the imagination. Berkson does not deny alienation of a sort; the sto-ries that we tell ourselves—history in the bad sense—can prevent us from seeing the world with fresh eyes. But the return to childhood is itself one of the stories we tell ourselves, and it perpetuates our alienation by telling us that we have to recover a power we have lost, rather than simply rediscover a power we still have. At the conclusion of his 2006 lecture "The Uneven Phenomenon," Berkson flatly rejects the famous narrative of loss inscribed in Wordsworth's "Resolution and Independence": "We poets in our youth begin in gladness; / But thereof come in the end despondency and mad-ness" (*Sudden Address* 108). "My experience has run distinctly counter to what Wordsworth proposed as an eternal verity," Berkson declared. He proceeded to tell about Robert Creeley's response at the end of his life to skeptics who wondered why Creeley now chose to write poems that did not fit the "experimental" mold in which the narrative of his career had been cast. "Because I can!" Creeley replied simply, exulting in a power owned rather than lost, a freedom that is "not unimaginable," as Berkson slyly describes it in "History" (*Portrait and Dream* 35).

History in the bad sense inhibits freedom; it dictates. "The dictates of history are not of this world," Berkson states in the recent poem "Glass Hoist" (*Portrait and Dream* 283). But the world to which Berkson would turn our attention is not the world that Wordsworth shuns, subject to the dictates of "getting and spending." Nor is it the world of a childhood idyll never to be recaptured, as Berkson makes clear in another recent poem, "Landscape with Calm," dedicated to the filmmaker Nathaniel Dorsky:

> Light breath across the windshield
>   the first raindrop scuttles
>
> Mild of eye still goes by word
>   of mouth of world
>
> Your call to hold it
>   completely initiated culmination's not
>
> A childhood wish
>   interminably avoided
>
> But coming and going
>   the sight of things   (*Portrait and Dream* 313–14)

Things compose this world, and they are wholly present to sight, not "interminably" deferred like the childhood wish or the wish to see like a child. Adult seeing achieves culmination, but it is intermittent, "coming and going," because it is engaged in the continual dialectic between seeing and saying, phenomena and nominalism. Though "mild of eye" like the filmmaker, Berkson the poet "still goes by word / of mouth of world."

WORKS CITED

Berkson, Bill. *Our Friends Will Pass Among You Silently*. Woodacre, CA: Owl Press, 2007.

———. *Portrait and Dream: New and Selected Poems*. Minneapolis: Coffee House Press, 2009.

———. *Sudden Address: Selected Lectures, 1981–2006*. [Brooklyn, NY]: Cuneiform Press, 2007.

Berkson, Bill, and Bernadette Mayer. *What's Your Idea of a Good Time? Letters and Interviews, 1977–1985*. [Berkeley, CA]: Tuumba Press, 2006.

Koch, Kenneth. *The Collected Poems*. New York: Knopf, 2005.

O'Hara, Frank. *The Collected Poems*. Ed. Donald Allen. Rev. ed., Berkeley, CA: University of California Press, 1995.

Wordsworth, William. *Selected Poems and Prefaces*. Ed. Jack Stillinger. Boston: Houghton Mifflin—Riverside, 1965.

AMANDA JANE EICHER

I can't say I ever consciously tried to make Bill Berkson smile in the ten years we've known each other, but I'm always thrilled when it happens. Bill has been very much like a father to me, so when he smiles at something connected to me in any way, I feel proud. Our conversations tend to cover history, poetics, art, and social life in a way that is so casual as to exclude the act of trying. Which is not to say uncritical or only nice. Early on in our friendship, Bill asserted, "I want to be around to watch you grow up." For ten years our friendship has provided liberty and gumption for me to see what happens, whether that means projects spread across four continents, a network of collaborations that threatens to tangle up, or the frequent "cramming" and "dispersal" that Bill and his friend Larry Fagin have diagnosed in my practice from time to time. Something central to this practice is the presence of a lunch table somewhere in San Francisco where Bill and I can cross glances. We have spread the History Positioning System—a way of placing ourselves in time—among these tables, and by now we expect this system to return us to those tables occasionally—or else, frowns. Bill frowns on my absences, and on scattered lives, and I think sometimes on my tendency away from object making as my practice more and more engages human relationships as a basic medium. These six drawings are a direct result of a tendency back to objects and touch points—sketches from Bill speaking on video, cross-checked with readings of Bill's work that's been waiting for me at home for a while—a very nice place to come back to. In a moment of reflecting on what I would want to contribute from our friendship to a conversation about Bill Berkson in the world, I realized I was very actively drawn to the possibility of making Bill's smile.

from an email I wrote to Bill Berkson:

Certain French alchemists begin their work by collecting dew.
My idea of a good painting—I'll make it for you if I can:
without notice I'll come to your house in the very early morning
and wake you up, a thermos of hot coffee in hand.
We'll walk to a clearing with canvases scattered about,
horizontally stretched just above the grass.
In the morning light they'll glitter with dew—
We'll walk around talking and looking until it evaporates.
My idea of a good painting is also my idea of a good time.

STEVE EMERSON

A Sketch of the Bill Berkson I Know

"Can you hand me that long spoon
snorkeling out of the sink."

A term of tellingly frequent use (denotes a
sizeable offense): "Dour." Pronunciation: dewer.

Descriptive catalog of the poems would be instructive.
The span is—well, it isn't a span. They hop around
occupying a quite large space with a strange shape.
They don't sort easily and the progression is not linear.
It isn't done to trip up the non-discerning. But it may.

Of Serge Chaloff: "You go
down. Where the money is."

After You

It is a very long walk
over hill and dale
and through the entertainment capitals of the world
to the dump.

A no-tolerance policy toward those who
showed up at his house with nothing to say.

Very very handsome.

Doing one-off copy-editing day work, encountered
with horror the following sentence:
"A weed isn't pretty, no matter how it looks."

"There's everything else, and there's me.
And my clothing."

Views on irony are complex and unsurprisingly
articulate. In three words: Yes and no.

> *old buttermilk sky*
> *going to the big city*
> *bye bye*

In a note, Schumann is "Schooby-doo."

Against the disease: fierce and graceful beyond
accounting.

Lots of small poems that glitter, or don't glitter, and
if they exist in time at all is because of the suddenness
of their stop. They do not convey. They please.

Around the middle of his person: a red belt.

"The middlebrow must not be tolerated."

LARRY FAGIN

The Bill Berkson Story

I discovered some bran macaroons, Sunshine,
You can buy in the supermarket, Finest,
But they're Sunshine, which reminds me
Of what Norman Winston said in the Hôtel de Paris,
Monte Carlo, at a party given by Elsa (dinner) Maxwell,
And I sat one person away from Noël Coward (I have a
Photograph). Garbo was there, too, and I was . . . it was
Great. We had this dog-faced waiter and Norman asked
"Do you have any macaroons?" The waiter
Couldn't believe it. He called for the maître d'
Who had a batch macaroons made up special but it took
1/2 hr (we had coffee). John Gunther was speaking.
Norman built the shopping center where Larry Rivers'
Mural is hanging I think (out in Smithtown) and . . .

JOHN GODFREY

For Bill

Urbanity was what I expected. I had read a borrowed *Saturday Night*—by
the time I was onto Tibor de Nagy books, it was unavailable—and, young
as I was, I imagined him in the context of Stardust New York, the art and
poetry world dating from the great Fifties, as a young man who was close
to the flame. The myths were very strong then. The upscale post-gallery
and post-reading parties of the day were remarkably open to coattailers
like myself, still in college, usually with my classmate John Koethe. At
such a party, fall of '66, someone pointed Bill out to me. I didn't expect the
model-quality handsomeness. His attire had the Fifties look, fine and tradi-
tional, as did his hair. I was an educated rube out of the upper lower mid-
dle class. I'd had years of free elite education among fellows who had been
raised in cosmopolitan and cultured homes. They possessed a confidence
and decisiveness I longed to have had. And that was my first impression of
Bill, and, of course, I envied him.

In March of '68 I was introduced to Bill at a Sunday morning, 11 a.m.
reading by John Wieners in the baggage room (attic) of the Hotel Albert.
Bill was gracious and welcoming to conversation. I was nervous, he was
kind, and the conversation was brief. I sat on a footlocker adjacent to the
one he sat on, and I felt, what a classy guy.

After a year in San Francisco, I returned to the East Village in autumn
of '69. Bill had a small but contemporary—I mean it wasn't a tenement—
apartment on 10th Street. Jim Carroll took me there. Apparently, you sim-
ply went over anytime until late in the evening, rang Bill's bell, and hung
out. It was so. Bill now had shoulder-length hair and wore mod gear of
quality. I don't know how he tolerated the traffic. Visitors forever playing
rock on his Blaupunkt. Plaster Casters. People who needed a night's crash.
There he was, a man of standards learned from a prior generation, taking
up the choices of the young. A lot of serious talk went on. Bill always had a
way of bringing substance to any subject, however hazy the heads might be.
From evenings there I came away with writings and composers to check
out, and I learned from Bill that the artist is a special kind of student. He
knew how to use his greater erudition benevolently. Throughout eternity

he would be the most civilized person in the room, but no spotlight. The same way that his great generosity didn't call attention to itself.

Shortly into the Seventies, Bill moved to Northern California. I've never lived down a road from him. Never heard a lecture he curated. I only hear him read if it's in New York. I miss out on the extensive personal. I've kept track of his work, and we see each other in New York. I've learned of his esteem for my poems, something I wear like laurels.

Bill's poems are what it's about. In his early development Bill cultivated the European derivations of irony and the arbitrary. There is interiority that goes with writing in New York. *Portrait and Dream* is the only "selected and new" I have that is alive. But this is not a review, and I'm going to generalize. When Bill fully gets his own sense of direction, around the time of the move to California, his poems have a newer immediacy and connection to real surroundings. The sense of speculation, of questioning how far a poem can be from the strictly literary to be close to it. In *Portrait,* "Start Over" works like a hinge, a poem as quark in supposition, all possible stations at once. Multiple techniques and multiple depths. A poem making up its own mind. Then there are periods when the lines are short, the angularity of thought pronounced, and juxtaposition is information. Bill's "thought" stands up to examination. When the poem's intent seems it might "come from" an influence, Bill does it better. His diction demonstrates yet underplays erudition. He exercises a judicious subtlety in poetry's open ranges. His voice, equanimity on simmer, stands up and stays for real. In each reading his best poems are even better than remembered, warmer, more chances taken, and more revealing. High standards live.

Bill is forever young, a blessing for us.

THYRZA NICHOLS GOODEVE

Bill Berkson: Fingers at the Tip of His Words

> For Jim Barsness
> If anyone, surprised by its wingspan, looks
> for something to blame . . . it's just Language,
> playing. Words, all by themselves, light each
> other up on the sides that are known as the
> rarest or meaningful only for the spirit, the
> center of vibratory suspense . . ."
>
> —STÉPHANE MALLARMÉ (235)

This is about Bill Berkson.

This is about a poet and art writing and technique as a form of moral integrity. It is also about friendship and love (as a discourse or "pump"[1]) and art and the word, as they are lived and acted upon by a person who is emblematic of what is necessary for the writer on art, a craft unfortunately set too far into the recesses of academe or under the neon glitz of money magazine deadlines, rather than in that "vibratory suspense" of language described by Roland Barthes as a skin. "Language is a skin: I rub my language against the other. It is as if I had words instead of fingers, or fingers instead at the tip of my words."[2]

Berkson is a poet whose language is always at the tip of his fingers. He uses the word as a site of negotiation and exchange, where organism and world call and respond to atmospheres, temperatures, and climates, articulating as they go, the knowledge and record of a life lived among others. Language and art entwine, under the sign of intimacy and sociality, like a couple whose skin has become one.

Of course, this is because he is a poet first, but as you read the following statement, replace *poetry* with *art writing*, *poem* with *essay*:

> In poetry [art writing], for it to work, both reader and writer need
> to be aware that every word counts (for or against the poem [essay],

---

1. One of those words only Berkson has found a way around: "Every season has its test of faith administered by at least one artist perceived as the exception who might just be delivering goods, or at least keeping the pumps from going altogether dry. (For 'pump,' read 'discourse'; for what is pumped, read 'meaning')" ("Critical Reflections," *SSM* 6).

2. "The point, no form of behavior exists exclusively. Maybe image making is the closest thing to writing. Painting has a skin" ("Poetry and Painting," *SA* 14).

that is). A poem [essay] is built word for word, one then another, like frame by frame, shot by shot, in a film. Without dictating an author-itative point of view, a poem [essay] can tell (like beads) the words—phrases you can turn here or there towards what might want to be said. That's part of poetry's [art writing's] sensational impact, where, at the edges of meaning, words return to their peculiar physicality (which then provokes undreamed-of connotations). It occurs to me that this sensation business, maybe because it was so much in the air for the painters at the time, has been with me from when I began to write seriously. ("Divine Conversation," *FOA* 21)

In other words, this "business of sensation" is what pulls the writing from the art and makes the art turn into writing. There are no boundaries, but a field of mutual inductions. Attentive to each detail (like the lover), each word, or each curve and flick of the line, at the edges of meaning . . . pro-vokes undreamed-of connotations. Like the beloved who both protects and won't let us get away with bad behavior, because every word counts, Berk-son's writing draws us—his "addressees"—into the art with care, respect, fidelity, so that we become extensions and participants. Art as a process of trust (of language) and intimacy (with the art).

The phrase he uses half-jokingly to describe himself is "the forlorn aes-thete."[3] The aesthete "proceeds, by stumbles and veers, along the lines of articulated sensations, cultivating a shifting horde of passions, tolerances, fascinations, glees, and disgusts that mark the temporary side effects of what keeps promising to be a civilized habit" ("Critical Reflections," *SSM* 5–6). Sounds like love to me, not sloppy silly fly-by-night infatuation, but love as a specific kind of knowledge of the other; where even in discord a special kind of insight drives the passion. Berkson uses language like the intimate who knows exactly what pressure points to push—art writing as a shifting horde of passions, tolerances, fascinations, glees, and disgusts.

Listen to Berkson when dyspeptic and annoyed: "Political iconography regularly takes on the narcissistic assurance of an exotic plant life; either cloying or laboriously thought up, it represents an indigestion of reality" (Garcia, *FOA* 41). Only disappointed love could cast a portrait as mocking, funny, precise, and evocative as this. You can't hate art or writing to talk

---

3. "As a poet/critic I often typecast myself for the purposes of argument as a more or less forlorn aesthete" ("Critical Reflections," *SSM* 5).

like this. That is because although he is an outsider ("I am an amateur on the scale of amateur-professional in an age of hyper-professionalization" ["No One Who Knows Me," *FOA* 278]), he writes from the inside. We experience the work through him like a bodily exchange. Here he is on Vermeer's milkmaid:

> Leaning gently into her task, this astonishing barrel of a woman shifts her weight away from the splendid, though nowise pristine white wall, lips parted in a smile as the earthenware pitcher releases a white skein from its rim. The smile holds its secret, murmuring, at one with the massive presence it seems key to. . . . Vermeer's maid appears in the middle distance in the guise of a sort of lunar blessing. She is strength and help, appetite and caution, warmth and removal, privacy, decorum, daydream and delight. . . . Contour-defining light at the right edge of her frame is augmented by skitters of white paint down the silhouette, a device Vermeer resorted to mostly early on. . . . The whole scene centers, subtly, teetering, on her waist. ("The Visitor," *FOA* 248–49)

There is care in there, attentiveness transformed into "perceptual confrontation."[4] He doesn't write *on* an artwork or an artist but *with* and *inside*. Listen to the materials in these descriptions, the merging of language and object, the loss of boundary between the visual and linguistic:

> Kline simplified but allowed plenty of noise. His hard finishes show a permeability to vision like the night air. His directional lines make for dual sensations of passage and grip. . . . A black-and-white line surface gathers sharply and wells towards the observer; moored to the edges it nudges them to expand. The blacks connect to edges or to other blacks, while the whites divide and scintillate. Black and white surface gathers sharply and wells towards the observer; moored to the edges or to other blacks, while the whites divide and scintillate. Black and white together or separately careen edge to edge as prodigiously as stretched lines. There are things white does black will never do,

4. "Artists are educated mostly away from where the art is; they know art—as do the art-history majors who become career critics—by theory and slides, rather than perceptual confrontation" ("Critical Reflections," *SSM* 7).

and the other way around, like consonants and vowels. ("Kline's True Colors," *SSM* 24)

The paint is a verb, described with an essential accuracy, down to the detail. As he is speaking about de Kooning, white turns into a synesthetic display, drawn from his insight into the everyday practice of the artist:

> White, when posited as a color rather than as a colorless ground, is always forward. Among the whites here are deep mists and dry glares, finely shaded alabaster membranes and swansdown plumage, brimming creams, spumes, and the taffy-like laminates and florid glosses that result from loading tube colors. ("De Kooning," *SSM* 147)

Hell . . . membranes, creams, and taffy, just the "ordinary artist"[5] working from his paint tube. But dignity and revelation are everywhere—even in the grummy glung of iridescence produced by the ballpoint pen:

> The ballpoint's thin, reiterative contour strokes pool up slowly, a process that both goes with and against the nature of the tool. Ballpoint pens are designed for speed and fluency on paper, ... ballpoint ink oxidizes, leaving an iridescence like that of a grease puddle on a dirt road, deep dazzle. If the blue ink sidles up to gold leaf in a sweet reprise of 14th century spiritual glamour, it's no accident. Barsness is after exactly that passage from one human affirmation to the next. ("Jim Barsness," *FOA* 90)

Has ballpoint pen ever had a better street hawker?

In these descriptions Berkson reminds me of that visionary man of language in the name of the inarticulable, Antonin Artaud, writing on Van Gogh in one of the greatest pieces of art writing of all time:

> I will tell you that Van Gogh is a painter because he has reassembled nature, because he has, as it were, perspired it and made it sweat, because he has spurted on to his canvases in heaps, monumental with

---

5. "An important figure in my mythology of art making is the Ordinary Artist. The Ordinary Artist is the one who just does his job. No sweat. The Ordinary Artist does whatever comes to hand along with an everyday will to art" ("For the Ordinary Artist," *FOA* 218).

colours, the centuries-old struggle of elements, the terrible rudimen-
tary pressure of apostrophes, stripes, commas and strokes, of which
we must admit that, after him, natural appearances are made. (48)

Berkson's acute, well-tended ekphrasis excels precisely where many fail—
when writing about the "no-image," the blank, or the canvas of pure
abstraction.

> At sixty-two, Mitchell continues to advance a naturalistic mode of
> improvisational abstract painting in its most limber extensions. She
> synthesizes effects of landscape and other recollected sensations and
> expands upon them in flashes and tangles of paint. ("In Living Chaos,"
> *SSM* 69)

Berkson, as is well known, "grew up" with painters, and the affective
relations he has maintained with the painter as "ordinary artist" are every-
where. In his descriptions of first encounters with painters, the sense of
identification is immediate:

> In New York, then, the signal gesture was de Kooning's expansiveness
> and speed, which suggested spatially the kind of surface excitement
> poetry was beginning to take on as well. A year later, seeing Philip
> Guston's work—especially his drawings with their slower accumula-
> tion of image—I was struck in a different way. The mass-effect of his
> line was more like a confirmation. In the case of de Kooning I felt,
> "Oh God, I'd love to write like that," but I'd have to hurry up. I wasn't
> fluent at that level. Whereas, with Guston I felt "I do write like that"—
> having some inkling of his process, a fellow inchworm! ("Poetry and
> Painting," *SA* 17)

"Inchworm" may be one way of putting it, but the painter in him takes off
from the same platform as the poet: with the word. In essays such as "Sweet
Logos," on Ed Ruscha, or "DeKooning, with Attitude," he turns the singular
word into a swatch and travels with it down its etymological roots, scraping
and layering, creating in some instances near-etymological odes.[6] This is

6. The funniest and best is too long to quote here but can be found in his essay on Dante
where he riffs off of the "sublime" ("Idealism and Conceit," *SA* 49–51). A tour de force, it is
hilarious and brilliant all at once.

done to special effect in "DeKooning, with Attitude." "I have to have an attitude," says de Kooning (referring to what he believes artists fill abstract space with). Most writers would carry on from there, leaving "attitude" to just sway in the breeze because, of course, we all know what an attitude is. Not so with Berkson:

> . . . it should be obvious that de Kooning didn't intend "attitude" in the more recent, negative sense of affecting a nastily argumentative stance. DeKooning's sense, I believe, is closer to the one in classi-cal dance vocabulary having to do with how parts of the body are arranged: for example, lifting the body from the toes of one foot, up and outward, with one leg out behind and bent—a balancing act, like Mercury's classic one, that lasts only a couple of seconds or it has to be regained. Or else, and more to the point (from Webster's Tenth): "a . . . state of readiness to respond in a characteristic way to a stimulus (an object, concept or situation)." (150–51)

Language is an opportunity, the locus of expansion and visualization, "a balancing act, like Mercury's classic one," embodied with tension and geometry, just as de Kooning's thrusts into abstract space suggest. The image of the dancer pushes us off the page. *Attitude* has become not poetry but the work of the poet. "So etymology is a kind of crystal text, a transit system you can travel and get almost anywhere" ("Idealism and Conceit," *SA* 51), as Berkson pushes even further, quoting from Webster's itself: *Attitude* as "a state of readiness," a form of response "in a characteristic way to a stimulus (an object, concept or situation.)" The use of de Koon-ing's own phrase is part of the encouplement of art with artist that emerges from his experience; the "facts" of his absorption and integration in the life around him:

> I quote a great deal because things other people have said or written have become part of my experience, and to that extent, are there for me to say and say again, as much part of my vocabulary as anything else I could possibly invent. ("Divine Conversation," *FOA* 11)

He does not cauterize quotes, using them as blocked-off separations. They exist within his text as indigenous grafts, shared and incorporated as one encompassing body. Experience as an ongoing conversation, with art, the world, poets, and friends, but most essentially the reader, the addressee. In other words, there is always someone there.

DIVINE CONVERSATION

> Rob startled me, quoting Whitman, then commenting on Whitman's, and, by extension, Nauman's, generosity, the open sociability of each towards the addressee: "The poet is interested in who you are."
> ("Divine Conversation," FOA 16)

I first heard "Divine Conversation: Art, Poetry and the Death of the Address" as a talk given at the School of Visual Arts several years ago. It is now republished in *For the Ordinary Artist* and serves, appropriately, as the gateway to the rest of the book. Since that time, I have read and reread the essay, sent it to numerous friends, and used it as the initial text in my class on art writing. When I first heard it in 2008, it was one of those talks that both glued me to and lifted me off my seat. Not only did it intersect and affirm so much of what art had always meant to me, but the opening paragraph unknowingly tapped almost verbatim into a conversation I had just had with the artist Jim Barsness on the phone.

> My theme tonight is conversation—conversation and its disconnects, you might say—or discontents, of which I am maybe one, so tempting it is to become a scold (but I'll try to avoid that). Conversation may be the intense, extended talk people generate among themselves, a kind of telepathy between the things some people do and those others who don't but find them interesting to confront, and then the things that follow from that, and so on, everywhere. I mean, the ongoing exchange, like of gasses in and out of the body, that you hope never ends and know to be brief, unruly and meant to be enjoyed as such. (11)

The theme of "telepathy," in friendship, of conversation "you hope never ends," as "gasses in and out of the body" was precisely what had been spoken between me and Barsness that week, as if our private "ongoing exchange" between writer and artist was now being channeled through

Bill, who was up there reminding us at that very moment how art is about not just looking at objects but looking within the context of a series of relations—risks between you and me— "a field or social gathering."[7]

As he put it,

> "Continue the conversation" is a prompt I've heard more or less at my back for most of my writing life. The phrase implies a continuum of art as a field or social gathering, across which possibilities move, change, emerge and reduplicate over time, not necessarily in chronological order, and with the understanding that no mode, old or new, can ever be said to be dead, as in utterly out of the question, snub it as you may. (11)

The conversation that never stops; the readiness of response within a field of others, "the open sociability . . . towards the addressee" (16) of art as "a continuum" defined as a "social gathering, where possibilities move, change, emerge and reduplicate over time, not necessarily in chronological order," where "no mode, old or new, can ever be said to be dead. . . ." (11)

"Divine Conversation" brings together everything that makes Berkson so singular as well as what makes art writing, at its best, no simple act of criticism but an exegesis on our lives in art, as well as the role art has in our lives as an action, a behavior, a "moral image"—a phrase from Edwin Denby that Berkson says he has returned to again and again:

> Talking to Bill and to Rudy for many years, I found I did not see with a painter's eye. For me the after-image (as Elaine de Kooning has called it) became one of the ways people behave together, that is, a moral image. (19)

Language as a skin that is rubbed, fingers at the tips of words, gasses in and out of bodies. Poussin unfolds "as you look, and as you look to comment on it, or listen, to whoever is looking alongside you at the same time, too." Here is the readiness and response to an object or situation as a quality of attitude—the attitude of the lover (writer) and beloved (language, art, friends) in their everyday exchange. And from this, what Berkson receives

---

7. This is a quote from Yvonne Rainer's film *Journeys from Berlin/1971* (1980). It sums up the relationship between artist and viewer, writer and reader.

is "the beauty, order and passion generated from talk and mutual contemplation itself." Not power conversations, not academic gamesmanship, or art world finagling, but "looking with educated eyes" and contemplation, self and other, where mutuality, cast in the everyday, is what produces the "vibratory suspense" of revelation.

So, a note scribbled to myself in the midst of Rives's and my exchanges:

> A Quoi Bon, asks Baudelaire in the Salon of 1846
> (Well, OK, he asks this of art criticism,
> but he has just
> finished an equally profitless boosting
> of art to deaf middle-class ears.)
> What's the good?

> Le Bonheur de Vie, says Matisse
> —not in fact some remotest Age d'Or but that
> we have bodies;
> there are trees and water and light and air
> —and art.
> All sustaining things
> accessible via senses
> as such primordial
> (hence, Golden,
> even, arguably, good).   ("Divine Conversation," *FOA* 14)

WORKS CITED

Artaud, Antonin. "Van Gogh, The Suicide Provoked by Society." Paris: Éditions Gallimard, 1947. Reprinted, http://monoskop.org/images/9/9b/Artaud_Antonin_Van_Gogh_the _Suicide_Provoked_by_Society.pdf.

Berkson, Bill. "Critical Reflections." 1990. *The Sweet Singer of Modernism & Other Art Writings, 1985–2003.* Jamestown, RI: Qua, 2003. (abbreviated *SSM*)

———. "De Kooning, with Attitude." 1999/2000. *SSM*. 150–55.

———. "Divine Conversation: Art, Poetry and the Death of the Address." 2008. *For the Ordinary Artist: Short Reviews, Occasional Pieces & More.* Buffalo, NY: BlazeVox, 2010. *FOA*. 11–22.

———. "For the Ordinary Artist." 1990. *FOA*. 217–18.

———. "Idealism and Conceit (Dante's Book of Thought)." 1984. *Sudden Address, Selected Lectures, 1981–2006.* [Brooklyn, NY]: Cuneiform, 2007. 35–56. (abbreviated *SA*)

———. "In Living Chaos." 1988. *SSM*. 69–74.

———. "Jim Barsness." *Artforum*. October 1990. Reprinted, *FOA*. 90–91.

———. "Kline's True Colors." 1986. *SSM*. 20–26.

———. "No One Who Knows Me or My Writing Will Believe It." 2010. *FOA*. 276–81.

———. "Poetry and Painting." 2007. *SA*. 13–23.

———. "The Visitor: Vermeer's Milkmaid at the Met." 2009. *FOA*. 248–250.

Garcia, Rupert. *Artforum*. December 1986. Reprinted, *FOA*. 40–41.

Mallarmé, Stéphane. "The Mystery in Letters." *Divagations*. Trans. Barbara Johnson. Cambridge, MA: Belknap Press of Harvard University, 2007. 231–36.

SYLVIE GORELICK

A Note to Bill

Dividing time
between a poem and the East
I find a glint of you
discovering America
one morning
breaking and entering
and beating revelation at its game
the task is numerous and early
an old cathedral's window at
the opening of your heart
that newly crowned me
independence, Bay Ridge avenue and
wrestling
have caught me unawares
and it is drinking season,
football season
stores closing early
and the season subsides
gives way to us
the worm in blood
as we go forth

Bill's Hands

my coffee cup runneth over
I am scalded
drink it black
it's dirty

the sun also slants
mild on wet eyelids
I'm a block of ice
blocking you

we stumble out of the church
onto the glaring pavement
Bill's hand warm as feathers
opens the box selects a song
the snow isn't blue anymore
but blue is the meaning of Bill's eyes
the dead boy sat on a red chair
naked with violin
now his father is gone
too soon or near, far or never
Bill holds my eggshells in his hand
days of the week are egg-colored
or shades of fine ground green or yellow

names aren't good enough for colors
sun will lace up on monday
snow on tuesday it'll be lonely
my eyes follow deer
they prance
disappear quicker than grief
must every creature be immortal?
for instance I hopped
over a dead squirrel
victim of some internal shock

and Lucy threw up four times
daintily on wednesday
there is no future tonight
only appalling darkness
and the radiator

TED GREENWALD

13 3s for Bill B

Open with
Hit it off
Likewise

Good eye peels
A bell curve
A really nice note

Yangtse sidestroke
Keep smiling keep smiling
Here comes *a saying*

Riding an old peony
At first fall
Ball bangs backboard

Back inside
Gravelly crunches
Hazy hot humid

Cloud hint
Breeze *hint hint*
Traffic, almost no

Lyrics droop earward
Fast forward
Melt away dot good time

Sound of water
The old pond
Jumpy

Debrief candlelight
A daze *oh wow*
A fool lounge

A park in waiting
Room enough for *awe*
Full echo remake

Skid around
Learning curve
Fly out off

Locale smithies
Hammer out landscape
Cloud shadow greens

Dawn forever
Better Louie Louie
Let alone blues

JEFF GUNDERSON

"For Bill: Anything."

Let it be known…

that I, along with all others attached to this festschrift, emphasize our enthusiastic "Aloha" for the gift of heart (& lungs), wisdom, and glee given to us by Bill Berkson . . .

and whereas . . .

Bill Berkson, as a lover of libraries, and as a librarian's dream patron, has educated (with eloquence and elegance) the many—be they student, colleague, librarian—of the rich life of poems, art, words: poets and artists from Bladen to Baldessari to Brainard; Denby to Denes to DeFeo; O'Hara to Onslow-Ford to Oropallo; Gablik to Guston to Group Material; Padgett to Park to Pollock; Ringgold to Rivers to Ruscha; and Katz to Koch to Krazy Kat . . .

and moreover . . .

as an advocate of the written and spoken word; plus as inspiration for writers & poets evidenced so gracefully at the head of the long rectangular oak table in the reading room of the Anne Bremer Memorial Library encouraging in clockwise order rookie poets—his students—to ante-up fluent phrases and then in a second and third round raise and rise to their best poems and words . . .

and furthermore . . .

as Bill Berkson orchestrated and organized cerebral and celebratory summer art writing conferences sandwiched between Fall and Spring Artists Lectures (Art of Now!) spanning three (3!) decades along the northeastern slope of San Francisco's Russian Hill luring a stellar cast of hundreds including (among many others) poets, artists, critics, writers, historians: Ashbery, Alpers, Murray, E. de Kooning, Kruger, Puryear, Haring, Eggleston, Brakhage, Fischl, Thiebaud, Baltz, Sultan, Krauss, Coe, Fox, B. Saar, Chadwick, Bleckner, Export, Irwin, Buchloh, Piper, Nerdrum, Acconci, Ferris, Storr, Kelley, Heinecken, Rainer, Parks, Acker, Salle, Cage, Schneemann, Rosler, Kaprow, Snow, Spero, Weems, Meiselas, E. Kienholz,

N. Kienholz, Colescott, Rubins, Ryman, Hammons, A. Saar, Ligon, Kozl-off, Goldin, Hickey, Wilson, McClure, Whalen, Hyde, Hill, Jaar, Ocampo, Neshat, Hopps, Rauschenberg (but whatever happened to Basquiat?) . . . (whew!) . . .

and thus . . .

when asked to contribute for this collection another writer responded affirmatively and succinctly: "For Bill, *Anything*!" (Call & Response!) I will second that!

Therefore Let It Be Proclaimed, on this date in 2011, that Bill Berkson is brilliantly a part of our psyches and spirits and hearts and we are the much better for it!

And thus I call upon all good citizens of the art/poet/writer world to salute and bear hug, figuratively as well as literally, our good friend.

Jeff Gunderson
Librarian
SFAI

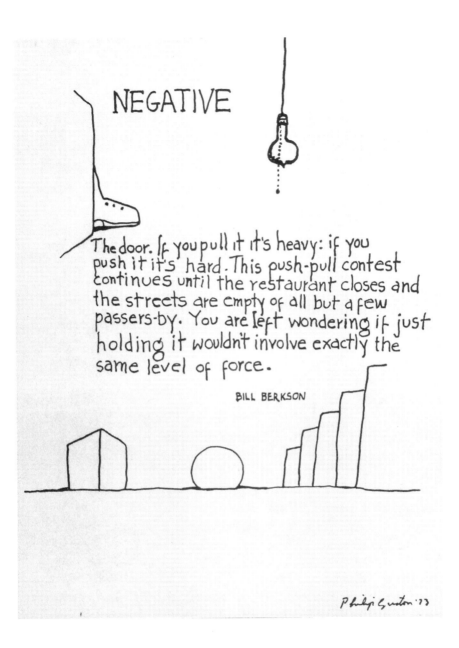

NEGATIVE

The door. If you pull it it's heavy: if you push it it's hard. This push-pull contest continues until the restaurant closes and the streets are empty of all but a few passers-by. You are left wondering if just holding it wouldn't involve exactly the same level of force.

BILL BERKSON

PHILIP GUSTON

DOUG HALL

For Madeleine, in Hitchcock's *Vertigo*, as for Nadja, in André Breton's novel of the same name, the city is an accumulation of those places that touched or concealed the body of a lover. These chimeras, objects of insane desire, haunt the psyches of the ones obsessed and turn areas of the city into erogenous zones. Even for those of us less possessed, the places we inhabit retain residue of—are haunted by—everything we experienced within them.

DIANE HALL

ANSELM HOLLO

From Hipponax
                    to Bill Berkson

I bow to Hermes

wait for the Sun to rise

in his bright shirt

YVONNE JACQUETTE

ALEX KATZ

VINCENT KATZ

Non Dimenticar: Bill Berkson as Poet, Editor, and Critic (2012)

Bill Berkson belongs to that identifiable species of writer known as the poet-critic. He has written and published both poetry and criticism from the early 1960s, when he was in his early twenties, thereby inviting comparison to Baudelaire, Apollinaire, Denby, O'Hara, Ashbery, Schuyler, and other top minds. It is challenging company, something to live up to, and represents a particular approach to the world. By and large, most poet-critics do not essay fiction or that other vehicle of potential lucre, biography. But if criticism is autobiography, then it all boils down to the shape of the writer's mind, what he or she has at the tip of his or her tongue.

Berkson began publishing criticism in Lita Hornick's *Kulchur* and in *ARTnews*, under the editorship of Thomas B. Hess. Both magazines were known for their hybrid natures, with poets writing about visual artists, artists writing about artists, poets writing about film, etc. Both presented opportunities for poets to exercise their critical muscles in a friendly, though demanding, editorial environment. *Kulchur* offered space as well for poets to publish their poetry. Over the years, Berkson has become known as one of our most trenchant art critics, period. He has long been a corresponding editor to *Art in America* and has been a frequent contributor to *Artforum*, *Aperture*, *Modern Painters*, and others. His critical work has been at the center of the arena. More recently, Berkson has written critical pieces that tie together his diverse interests, making manifest the connections he sees among various disciplines, including criticism itself.

In "Critical Reflections," published in 1990, Berkson makes some of his most cogent observations about the art of criticism. "The main point," he writes, "is to give people something to read, to be accurate about the work . . ." A central task of the critic, according to Berkson, is imagining a possible audience, thereby allowing him or her to develop a vocabulary both appropriate to the subject and particular to the writer. Later in the same essay, he returns to this idea of a new vocabulary: "Predictable language suits only an art with predictable meanings. If criticism has all the words in place—a fixed vocabulary—it has stopped looking and won't listen for the words that might be there for the work." The poet-critic offers a different approach from that of the theoretician, who works from established terminologies and taxonomies, fitting art work into those preexisting categories. Poet-critics call specific flavors to mind. As Berkson puts it, "Poets bring a technical proficiency to art writing as well as an attitude that, in art's increasingly institutional settings, seems proportionately ever more off the wall." One might add: "And called for!"

In "Divine Conversation: Art, Poetry and the Death of the Address," published in 2008, Berkson expands on the qualities that make poetry tick, particularly contemporary poetry, schooled in modernism's working modes, and how poetry might influence criticism:

> In poetry, for it to work, both reader and writer need to be aware that every word counts (for or against the poem, that is). A poem is built word for word, one then another, like frame by frame, shot by shot, in a film . . . at the edges of meaning, words return to their peculiar physicality (which then provokes undreamed-of connotations).

What is the audience for this careful, precise play with words? Although not by any means huge, still, Berkson argues, poetry's influence can be pervasive. He likens poetry to the scale of chamber music and cites Peter Schjeldahl's disavowal of poetry in favor of a perceived possibly greater public profile for the influential critic. In an interview with David Levi Strauss, published in 2006, Berkson remarks: "Poetry, as all the art people would tell you, is beside the point. No cultural currency, they say, because the attendance figures are so low. Phooey. Poetry strikes back, gloriously beside the point. It does its work and leaches into the general culture, which it seems to have done for the past millennium, practically." In a lecture delivered at the Skowhegan School of Painting and Sculpture in the same year, Berkson returns to this image: "Poetry . . . has its durable density, its fructifying nonsense, its interventions as subtle, as surreptitious as a leach field, its ingredients percolating through the common culture as we speak."

When we turn to Berkson's own poetry, we find a rich leaching field of its own that has certainly fed his critical practice. How do we characterize this poetic output, encompassing, now, some fifty years of published work? Berkson himself gives a clue in his 2006 Skowhegan lecture, when he affirms that "[t]he specific power of contemporary poetry may lie in its arcane randomness. . . . A poet's collected work over time will be usually

James Schuyler, Carl Morse, Alex Katz and Bill Berkson New Year's Eve 1962;
courtesy Alex Katz

about many different things, possessed of diverse effects, and often done in
different styles, even though the characteristic tone may be consistent." In
the same lecture, he specifies the difficulty poetry faces in today's particular
culture: "good poetry tends to be highly nuanced and nuance is not much
tolerated in the time famine that is today."

A particular group of publications by Berkson, from the late 1960s to the
mid-1980s—*Shining Leaves* (Angel Hair Books, 1969), *Recent Visitors* (Angel
Hair Books, 1973), *Enigma Variations* (Big Sky, 1975), *Saturday Night: Poems,
1960–61* (Sand Dollar, 1975), *Blue Is the Hero: Poems, 1960–1975* (L Publica-
tions, 1976), *Lush Life* (Z Press, 1984)—brought into one's consciousness an
awareness of Berkson's poetry as an ever-overlapping opening-up of a poet-
ics, based in the rolling waves of the New York School's surf, yet mellowing
out on the mesa of the poets' colony of Bolinas, California, recovering, as
it were, from the clamor and degradations of the big city's cutthroat modus
operandi, discovering a more open daily expanse.

Berkson's poetry has much of the randomness, the disjunctive quality,
he refers to in his Skowhegan lecture. In the early *Saturday Night* poems,
it is the randomness of youth, an almost *American Graffiti*–like quality of
modernism, in the wake—or rather, as they were close friends, the glow—
of O'Hara and Ashbery. It is the extreme youth of beach parties and alcohol
one intuits in the opening lines of Berkson's poem "Breath." Kenneth Koch,

Berkson's teacher at the New School, is available here too, in the out-of-breath, repeated exclamations with which the poem begins:

> November! November! Smoke outrunning branches, reefs
> turning hideous and cold, windows accepting porches
> accepting the draft, the dust, its vacancies like the arctic
> desert . . . the lead-dogs in heat, thirst of adventurers
> for elastic, the bench, walk, and fountain certainties!
> it is definitely a city like the top of something, the pole!

In the ensuing years, ever-greater senses of continuity will lead to some of Berkson's most memorable work. Not coincidentally, many of these poems coincide with Berkson's move from NYC to Bolinas. While it would remain New York School, Berkson's work evolved an evocative "1960s" sensibility in these years, as his became a voice in and for its time. Partially, one might argue, this had to do with the effect of Berkson's ever-deeper immersion in the visual art of his time on his poetry.

A simple, laconic poem, "Dark Cloudy Sky," signals the change. It is matter-of-fact, appropriated, almost, from the world. It could not have been written by O'Hara, Koch, or Ashbery. The closest NYS mentor would be Schuyler, but Schuyler would have added much verbal innuendo, whereas Berkson takes pains to avoid the slightest implication of personality.

The "classic" Berkson poems start to hit with "Booster," "Levantine," "Stanky," and continue with "Non Dimenticar," "Facing East," etc. In these poems, the plainest language possible—the language of "Dark Cloudy Sky"—is used to diverse emotional ends. "Booster" makes disaster domestic, negotiable, something one might see on television. "Levantine" remains opaque, and "Stanky" achieves liftoff via its extreme limitation—a hermetic poem that harbors a philosophical dynamo, ready to release, if the reader be ready to receive it. "Non Dimenticar" is more cinematic than "Dark Cloudy Sky." "The Bicycle Thief" is another type of poem. Theoretically similar to "Dark Cloudy Sky"—it takes a stance of straight documentation of observed phenomena—"Bicycle Thief" adds to that basic gambit the use of telling social document. It makes a statement by what it chooses to focus on—what De Sica's movie signified in the time and place of the poem's composition and publication. The poem functions as criticism-as-poetry, a particularly personal twist on bringing other forms of writing into one's poetics. The poet resists criticism per se, here restricting himself to description within the frame of experience ("I go see *The Bicycle Thief* . . . / The picture gets dimmer. The End.") Only one line can be considered *critical*, and it is the one on which the poem hinges: "Alfredo is the Bicycle Thief." This is a new type of poem, for Berkson, and for American poetry.

At this point, the persona in Berkson's poems, the "I," seems to have achieved a new comfortableness, and this results in poems of a surprising directness, such as "Brightness," dedicated to Berkson's friend Katie Schneeman. The rhythm in the poem is evinced in the line breaks. Phrases spaced out on the page—not to indicate breath exactly but to indicate *thought* pauses, the pauses again linked to a particular moment and way of thinking Berkson has become attuned to:

> Katie
>   you stay
> where everybody wants
> to be
>   very pretty   head straight
> & soft forward

By the late 1960s, Berkson had determined his characteristic modes, and he would expand on them throughout his career: the isolated memory (as in "From a Childhood," cp. Schuyler's "Milk") or thought ("In the Breeze"), the dream poem ("Dangerous Enemies," "Duchamp Dream," "Dream with Fred Astaire," etc.), the almost-concrete miniature ("Canto," "Levantine," Love Story," "Sudden Fear"), the personal poem ("Brightness," "Enigma Variations," "Vibration Society," "Traveler's Companion, "To Lynn," "Don't Knock It," "Song for Connie"), description-as-poem ("The Bicycle Thief"), account-as-poem ("The Red Devil," "Fourth Street, San Rafael"), the philo-sophical poem ("Stanky," "Nagative"), the rhythmic riff ("Brightness," "Roots").

And then there is the flux of Berksonianism that actually constitutes the majority of the lines in the poems. This is dense, turgid, verbiage—poetry to be sure, not prose, particular poetry by a particular artist, whose work has become beloved even as it, in these turns, remains difficult of access. So, by this point in the road, does it still make sense to say New York?

What the hell, yeah, because it's always there, in so many ways—personal, professional, artistic (Fred Astaire was New York too, growing up with the Gershwins, as was Humphrey Bogart, who briefly attended Berkson's alma mater, the Trinity School, as did Jim Carroll and Aram Saroyan). But Bill is a poet of the world, as beloved in Paris as in San Francisco, and part of his worldliness is that willful difficulty.

For this reader, the most powerful of Berkson's poetry occurs when he's found a way to boil down the experimental into a *connection*—usually with a person, sometimes to a memory or present observation. This happens swiftly in "Red Devil," heartbreakingly in "Traveler's Companion," coolly in "Fourth Street, San Rafael," and mysteriously, yet unwaveringly, in "Song for Connie":

> Love shapes the heart
>   that once was pieces
>
> You take in hand
>   the heart in mind
>
>   Your fate's consistent
>   alongside mine

In Berkson's criticism, one is always aware of the long view, of Dante and Titian, as much as R. Crumb and Richard Prince, while in his poetry the feeling is always of the present tense, even in the memory pieces. Time's vagaries take from us those whose lives have defined us. That certainly happened to Berkson, beginning with O'Hara, and yet we see in Berkson's work his definition of the life of a writer, an attempt to react to that loss, not to take it sitting down, so to speak, but to stand up for the right to make sense of that loss. In his Skowhegan lecture, Berkson put this into clear perspective: "Artists you know as friends and heroes and teachers die, you miss their company, and what compensation there is, large enough to matter, arrives in the form of a wider, deeper—larger than life, one would almost venture to say—sense of their work, what it amounts to, where they took it, and how increasingly distinct as well as necessary it feels to be." *Distinct* and *necessary* are two words that easily apply to all Bill Berkson has provided us, over all these years, using a poet's ear to determine the vocabulary that enriches the critic's observations.

KEVIN KILLIAN

Up to the Sky

I remember only one time when I wanted an airplane flight to last longer. Well, there was the time when my wife and I saw the actor John Travolta disappear into the first-class lounge in front of us, and we waited in anticipation for him to return, and he did, stepping amiably on our feet as the first one out. Somebody on the plane said that Travolta, a licensed pilot, goes into the cockpit of every flight he's on, hangs out with the captain, gets a little gold crew badge from him, plucks it on whatever he's wearing. Sure enough, he was grinning a mile wide and wearing some sort of gold thing on his lapel. Could this really be true? This was before 9/11, and maybe now the cockpit doors are closed to Travolta's grin, no matter how appealing, how controlling. But the story I want to tell is how, in October 2006, at SFO I got on what I assumed would be a boring flight to LA. My diary says it was October 21st. I was alone, had nothing good to read, etc., only the inflight magazine to look forward to; and then who did I see in the lounge when they called our boarding but Bill Berkson. "Are *you* going to LA?" I asked, incredulously, as though it were some sort of miracle. Apparently, he was going to visit his son, who was—now I can't remember what Moses was doing. On the plane we sat together, and I had the privilege of Berkson's undivided attention for seventy-two minutes. It was sheer heaven. The stewardess told us that weather problems in some other Western airport location were delaying all flights, and I was all smiles, just digging myself in and asking Berkson a good couple dozen of the questions I always save for him. What did he think of this, that, or the other. I'm trying to be more precise. Like the best conversationalists, he has a knack for making one feel totally listened to, and the gift of remembering exactly the most intriguing thing he's heard about you lately from a third party. My grandmother used to call this a "Trade Last"—a "T.L." for short. "So I told Myrna I had a good T.L. for her, since Sally told me that Myrna plays bridge better than most bridge pros." The point of a Trade Last is that once someone's compliment has been regaled to you, you must then return the favor by telling the first party something nice you've heard about them from others. Well, I wish my grandma had met Bill Berkson, for he is the master. "Now who was it mentioning your name to me, Kevin?" He'll sit there and think and then it will come to him—some wildly unlikely name. Jasper Johns. Lars von Trier. Whoever. I try to listen to people, but I don't do it as naturally as Berkson does—bringing in a larger world and yet locating you on it somehow, a butterfly on a girder. The point is that if you are going to give a Trade Last, give it the Bill Berkson way, be generous, astute—show your love. The truth is that we disagree vehemently on some matters, but if you ever find yourself in an airport waiting lounge with this man, you will soon be pinching yourself, thinking, now I know what it must have been like to be present at the table talk of Coleridge, Wilde, Oscar Levant.

Bill Berkson's poems have all the satisfying sweetness and shockingness and strangeness that one could hardly ever expect to find together. Meeting these disparate qualities in his poetry, one is "turned around," as it were, so that one has to reread the poems to see what's wrong. It turns out that nothing is, and that in fact what Berkson has done is found a new way of being right. Or, as Ron Padgett put it, "Bill Berkson's writing is witty, musical, daily and deep, underpinned by a bracing integrity and shot through with gorgeous abstraction and other brilliant hookups between eye, ear, mind and heart." The way his poetry got this way must be by his having been writing it, day after day, or week after week, for almost, now, forty years. The poetry never deviates from what it seems mainly to take as its subject, which is the richness and surprisingness of things, when they make sense and when they don't. When they don't make sense provides gala occasion for finding the new sense that they do make, so the subject matter is endless since the answers are poetry not bombs that would eliminate all the beautiful stuff around that is being looked at. Among this beautiful stuff is the English language, which gets quite a workout in the poems. Often there is even the rare experience of hearing what is being said along with its particular manner of being said at the same time and in a particularly satisfying way.

JOANNE KYGER

Rainy Tuesday

Our self idling in a moody moment
"Why did you want to go there anyway?"

Through the earnest rain in the backwaters
of Elephant Avenue before fences,
I hear the murmurous thoughts
of yesterday   Isn't it lucky
we don't need any lights
to find the path between two streets
Our feet know the way through the scrub
of the coastal zone   Once more
I wander in the light rain and wind
The Democrats are voting in New Hampshire
the troops are being decimated in Iraq
cows are still eating dead cows
And we're supposed to enjoy it?
I hear the voices of the underbrush
they sound like quail highly agitated
Which is all true
and genuine as your milky white hair
glowing under Aquarian skies

> January 27, 2004
> for Neighbor Bill

HARRY MATHEWS

A Bill Berkson Primer

"Trying to understand what it is actually like."

As a lady takes a doughnut from a car trunk
between thumb and forefinger, the perceptual moment clicks:
crumbs and contouring in an antique frame,
days when the dictates of grimy angels perspire
esperanto études at Weather Wall
(fuzzy shadow on the wall of someone chewing gum).
Glad hums in lunar abatement grace the rim
headed down the demon slopes
instead of standing still and growing upwards,
just as "lusts" make clear mimetic physics
knowing the babble that toil concludes, condones.
Looked into a photo saw the face gaunt going,
magnifying real cottage brands of stasis:
night the one color of a vocalist's shirt
or else my superstitions are wrong.
Perpetually stained it looks like home—
quizzical pink petals in a vortex of Oreos
recruited to receive pronouncements of the final
sound as a heart in love with darkness,
the sudden final adequacy of everything.
Unconditional surrender is the final solution,
Valence the face of the richly bearded god.
We're alive, you do alarm me to the fact,
xeroxing Sinatra's "Saturday night is the loveliest,"
yawning through the back yard and appointments and rain,
zigguratic high notes, chomps
around a rusty nail, sweet denim moon swallowed up;
but you are a champion of equidistant parts, you
compound the sands they shift and bare the foot-
drop, the simple click of the elevator cab.
Effortless stylishness regulates the enchanting
Fur—fur for steel as ourselves. Run it on your fingertip grate,

go from that to the nearest consolation.
Horns say "Late Summer"—
it is whiter than your face when I opened your icebox.
Joy to talk of paints: "Different schools," says Paul,
knowing the babble that toil concludes, condones,
moves along, dreaming, um, "wherever you are."
No, the words stay put, like dreams
of your words as they pass, as I do not hear them:
piquant muted red of spaghetti sauce,
régime change, permanent and without end.
So Lady Luck lets drop another of her interminable fireballs
upon a peak, and Boston is a bay. Honey dumps the flood (a
sunny world of doodling idiots),
the rest of us inhabiting our typical morass together,
you can't see it no matter how you magnify it—a god's-eye
view, which must finally be your own, the real one. A
wait for lunar task / Take the bait for lunar task,
xylophone tapped across a calm reflective stream:
you smooth the wrinkles on the edge of night.
Zodiac: pause, and a chair sails past me into solar radiance.

Afternoon walks on in a delicious drifting
because just stepping out into sunlight—
do things go further in need than I could? Or are they immune
in my own cage of marble and stool benches?
Someone behind the cello, wretchedly scherzo
to imagine vapors crossing the grid's white string
where the ashes of ordinary sparks fire again and again.

Bidding him drink of the inland sparkling sea:
"I didn't think you'd break that cup."
Telepathy between events, good times over too soon.
The small boy rolls some marbles around.
The table gets rounder than was guessed.
The world is waiting for the sun to rise.
They look everywhere. They stand in the rain, waiting.
Without being completely satisfactory, this is all.

BERNADETTE MAYER

Bill Berkson Memoir

I first met Bill at an auspicious gathering of . . . no, I met Bill long before that. I was taking a poetry class at the New School. I knew who Kenneth Koch was, but *Saturday Night: Poems*, by Bill, was beyond me, so I figured I should take his course; I was entranced by Bill's freckles and when he brought in piles of books by Ezra Pound and T. S. Eliot, showing us the difference in their heights. I remember Bill asking us what was distortion in poetry and I said, if you have a lot of thin letters like l's and I's, maybe that was distortion. The first time I ever visited Bill at his ancestral home, he was sleeping in the blueberry room; there were hotdogs in the fridge and nothing else. These rich people are weird, I thought. Later, when I visited Bill at his 57th Street apartment, he said, "Do you know where you are?"

Anyway, later Bill had a party for his "best" students and invited all the famous New York School poets, so I got to meet Frank O'Hara just before he died and John Ashbery, James Schuyler, Lee Harwood, and Jim Carroll. Later, at Bill's ancestral home, I discovered that the elevator opened right into his apartment and some dude would come up and ask what you'd like to drink. Of course, in those circles you'd drink a Negroni, which was a Campari and soda with vodka, but Joe Brainard would drink what we now call a Joe Brainard, which was without the vodka.

To me, at that time, this was my introduction to the world of grown-ups, or grown-up New York poets. It seemed they were mostly gay and rich. If they weren't gay, they were rich, but sometimes they were gay and rich. I always felt comfortable with gay and/or rich people, starting in college where I hung out with the "day students." It always made sense to me to have an astonishing wine cellar, a runway in your backyard, buttons to press if you needed salt or pepper. But why? Frances LeFevre once said to me, "You think the world owes you a living," but it wasn't me but everyone. I always cottoned to the idea of a guaranteed annual income. It doesn't make sense to be poor as a church mouse nor rich as crocuses. You'd think the day students would be the poorer ones, but not at the College of New Rochelle. Among the bridge players in the student lounge, I met a young woman who followed Bo Diddley around in her white convertible Thunderbird. Her father was the head of Berlitz. We played with another woman who had one sweater in all the different colors; she was related to Cardinal Spellman and had a "de" name followed by "saint." We all drank a lot and visited friends who'd been in car accidents. I don't think we ever did anything repeatable to a person with morals.

I left the College of New Rochelle as soon as my uncle died because they had been importuning me for reading Freud. At all the schools of Catholic origin I'd been to, I got into "trouble" for reading books, so it was nice to go to the New School. Anyway, I continued to hang out with Bill long after we both left that school. He married or lived with Lynn O'Hare, who is the person who gave birth to Moses. I was pregnant with Marie then, so Lynn and I began a correspondence about our pregnancies. When we all wound up at Naropa at the same time, I said to Bill, "I've never seen anybody bring so many clothes for one week." Bill said, "I think Lynn looks like a million dollars." Moses and Marie were both being toilet trained, so they would stop together to defecate beneath various trees on campus.

All this while, Bill and I were corresponding in what would be the book *What's Your Idea of a Good Time?* Also Bill published, as a Big Sky book, two lecture/readings from the *Studying Hunger Journals*. Later Bill said he didn't know there was more. I guess I was embarrassed to tell him.

Lately, if I get to see Bill, we enjoy getting our senior citizens discounts for museums. I love to look at painting with Bill but he's still a little out of my real. I am Bill's oldest friend and we both know what decorum is. I like Bill's clothes and his poems.

BEN MAZER

Bill Berkson and the Baby Spiders

> Thousands of tiny red pulsating baby spiders dropping down
> on me like parachutes over Japan
>
> "You ARE Howard Hughes."
>
> It's spring! no, summer! And Bill Berkson is at the top of my
> stack, and I am at the top of his stack, and it was Halloween,
> and you were on the telephone, and I was excited to see you
>
> "Hugo Flake!"

Bill is super fun, and super real, and that's how I know him. There is no way I couldn't get a kick out of his poems or listening to him read them. When Landis Everson had his stroke while visiting me in Boston (April 2006) and had to go into Mass General, I had to take his place, and it was electric to give a doubleheader with Bill at Harvard University. Bill is nothing if not gracious (and fun, and real), and we had a good talk about our Russian Jewish ancestry and the possibility of whether Bill ever knew my mother back at Brown University in the late fifties. We even talked about Mary Desti! This was on the way from Bill's hotel to take the train to visit Landis at MGH. Landis was in a bad way when we got there and was convinced that he was surrounded by cannibals who were planning on cooking him in a stew. As the nurses and doctors passed in and out of his hospital room, he inquired of them, "Are you all in a play?" Bill gave Landis that nice illustrated edition of *In Memory of My Feelings*, and also a copy of Bill's *Fugue State*, which Landis looked at carefully and, reading the cover, pronounced, "Hugo Flake!"—a story that Bill recounted with warmth and gusto at the Landis Everson Memorial at St. Mark's Church in January 2008. Another time I came out to San Francisco to give a reading, and Bill had the wonderful idea that we get haircuts together just before the reading. What could be more silly and fun! A day or two later Bill had me meet him over at his house on Grand View. I saw the famous crushed pack of Marlboro Reds on the wall, and Bill took me in the car to a nice restaurant where we had seafood and pasta, and talked about editing and writing for magazines like *Fulcrum* and *Culture*. Then Bill, ever gracious in wanting to show me a bit of local culture, dropped me off at that famous park—you San Franciscans know which one it is—where people just sit in droves on top of a big bare hill, looking down on the street or at the grass in front of their feet and taking in the sun. It wasn't difficult to find the ways and means of getting thoroughly baked in that friendly collection of idling students and locals! More recently, Bill came again to Boston, and we were invited to a dinner at Bill Corbett's. Bill and Connie were seated at the opposite head and at the opposite corner of the table, too far away for intimate speech, but Bill and I couldn't help giving each other little looks across the table. We had a good breakfast the next day, at the Cafe Algiers, and then Bill was off in a rented car to see Gerrit Lansing in Gloucester. I've read Bill's *Collected Poems—Portrait and Dream*—and they are great!—something distinctly American and distinctly Bill. We need to remember those poems as an integral part of our culture of the past fifty years. How much of the old New York is in them—Bill's childhood and the people he knew—but also how much of the strange, magnified, dynamically disorganized essence of American consciousness. Reading them, we (younger poets) can feel some sense—a sense at once physical and emotional—of what it might have been like in certain moments to have been Bill in Bolinas, or Bill anywhere out for a drive or a late-night lucubration. They are poems of passion and tenderness, of thoughtfulness, conscientiousness, whimsy and ebullience, and—yes—daring. They are fun, and they are real, and they are a part of us. That's why we love Bill!

DANIEL McNAUGHTON

"Strawberry Blond" by Bill Berkson

Knock on the forehead
there, there beach nothings
saw, reef, watery exchanges
of life O's not followed by
anything turf   True?
(ringlet)   (broadcast)
in wing around immortal portraits, are they?
the be-hanged cuneiform
money sniff)

rung ticker
a refusing passion
for burn on, brief nail!
under the sheets, a lip
hits the sulfur stripe
phone book being a strength
a) (its Irish sequel)
b) paralysis   mustard
back on the office
the rifting phlox
looks and wins
what cabinet of ruse and doubt
    gives him the possibility of love and honor through her eyes,
a doubtful sign of rain showing up on the back porch on which they swung
out the years of his death and on which she sat like an expectant mother—
    that
was unblackened!

Chocolate
Tiding over the grey embittered court

he prayed for his marriage
as was the modern custom   as if promiscuity were
    well, Stupid!   finding tics

What am I indicting that it breaks heads off gardenia?

> green green stovepipe
> arm around me stalk wherein pegged a relax bus
> globule of often-candelabra in the cake
> of soap she saw her face a few times
> feather in his blood
> margin   eat shit if
> in it old waterhole
> rub-down, shower, and melted
>
> in her sleep
>
> he woke up
>
> they went off   socks
>
> "Ain't no could be."

"Strawberry Blond" is a poem by Bill Berkson, written between 1959 and 1961, which appears in his recent book, *Portrait and Dream*. I find it very difficult to trace the train of thought in this poem as a whole: phrases seem to exist as discrete units, their relation to one another unclear more often than not. What's more, just getting a handle on where a phrase begins and ends in this poem is a tricky business. That turns out to be the poem's charm, however. What I admire about this poem is how much "could be" it contains. This is especially true in the first few lines of the first stanza, to which I will limit my discussion. I think these lines can be read, in terms of phrasing, in different ways, with corresponding alternative meanings. This is a happy ambiguity, as these meanings coexist without troubling one another.

The poem gets going with its title, "Strawberry Blond," which may or may not refer to either the "him" or the "her" of stanza 2, line 13. Typically, one would say a blond or any variation thereof is a woman, but this is not always true. Strawberry blond as a hair color is intermediate, being somewhere between red on the dark end of things and blond on the light end. Regardless of whether "Strawberry Blond" refers to anything contained in the poem, it certainly lets the reader know that he or she is in the realm of "could be," but not in any willful or peevish sense. This expression is not obscure or nonsensical—it is an expression in everyday speech.

The first line in stanza 1, "Knock on the forehead," seems straightforward enough, from a phrasing standpoint. It is worth noting, though, that "Knock" could either be a noun or an imperative, so things are unclear from the get-go. It's tempting to consider line and phrase as coterminous here—why not? Except that here comes line 2: "there, there beach nothings". Couldn't we treat the first word of line 2, "there," as the final word of the phrase begun in line 1 (and thus as a form of enjambment) because of the comma? As a phrase, "Knock on the forehead / there," makes sense, whether we take "Knock" as being the imperative of *to knock*, with "there" being part of telling the knocker where to knock, or we take "Knock" as a noun and "there," as merely clarifying where exactly the knock occurred.

Sure. On the other hand, "there, there" could be words of comfort to the person whose forehead is presumably sore. Yet then we get "beach nothings"—taken together, they recall "sweet nothings," with the long-*e* sound of "beach" recalling that of "sweet." Quite a shift in the type of intimacy here: we go from what a parent might say to a child ("there, there") to words between lovers ("beach nothings"). About those "beach nothings": if we keep it simple, line 2 reads "there, there beach nothings", with line and phrase being coterminous. Continuing on, line 3 begins "saw," apparently first in a list of items ("reef, watery exchanges"), if "saw" is taken as a noun. But what if it's not? What if it's the past tense of *to see*, and the comma that follows it means that "saw" actually completes the phrase begun on line 2 (another enjambment). So, using / to indicate a line break and // to indicate a possible phrase ending, one way of phrasing lines 1–3 (up to "saw,") would be: "Knock on the forehead / there, // there beach nothings / saw, //". In this case, the last note of phrase 1 ("there") is repeated to serve as the first note of phrase 2.

Let's stir things up some more. To this point we've assumed that "beach nothings" are a unit, and as long as we keep "saw," out of the picture, this is cool. "[S]aw," is trouble, however. If it is in fact the past tense of *to see*, couldn't "beach" be what "nothings" "saw"? Just as easily, though, couldn't "nothings" be what "beach" "saw"? But are we even certain that "saw" is the past tense of *see*? Couldn't it be the present tense of *to saw*? In this case, "nothings" must "saw" "beach"; we can't have "beach saw nothings". (Were Berkson writing in a heavily inflected language, needless to say, this sort of mayhem wouldn't ensue.) We're not done. "[S]aw" could be a noun as well; for that matter, "beach" could be a form of *to beach*. In that case, "nothings" "beach" "saw"—as above, the corollary isn't possible. "Saw beach nothings" is a no-go, since whatever form of *to beach* "beach" is, it is not the third-person singular.

Another reason we can't have "beach saw nothings" or "nothings beach saw" is that we don't. I've leaned on English grammar to pick my way through the first two lines of this poem, but respect for its laws can't trump respect for Berkson's aural syntax. Regardless of where I as the reader choose to end the phrases in this poem, from the point of view of sense (and an obscure sense of sense at that) "beach nothings saw" works musically. The phrase "beach saw nothings" is prosaic and frankly plodding, rhythmically, as it offers three strong accents in a row "beach saw no-things", whereas "beach no-things/saw" is lighter and syncopated. "[N]othings beach saw" is not so bad, actually, but it doesn't have the bounce of what we do have. "[B]each nothings saw" gives us a strong accent to let us know where we stand, then gives two quick syllables to render us either uncertain or at play—you choose—and finally a strong accent where we would expect a weak one, in the triple meter of this phrase. More on matters of meter later.

A reasonable person might say to all this that rather than chasing after these various possibilities of phrasing, wouldn't it be easier to track down a recording of Berkson reading the poem? Sure. After all, I'm no closer to attempting an understanding of this poem as a result of the foregoing discussion. But that wasn't my aim. What I've tried to do is lay bare what this poem does. It doesn't contain every single word in every single human (or nonhuman) language arranged in every possible sequence—the portion I have examined consists of eleven words (including the title), with one word ("there") being used twice. With these "limited" resources, however, "Strawberry Blond", at least in this very short section, can be phrased in more than one way by a reader with a reasonable grasp of English who happens upon it. That's the poem's charm and its meaning. The best way I can put it is that the poem is misleading, if the pejorative sense of *misleading* can be discarded. It's not that this poem is willfully obscure, that it withholds its meaning—it is evidence that meaning is constructed variously. "Ain't no could be" =

"could be".

p.s.: One of the most well-known characteristics of American poetry in the wake of Pound, so-called "free verse," is the abandonment of a regular foot. As has been pointed out, this doesn't mean that modern American poetry lacks rhythm. Williams attempted to get at what was going on with his "variable foot," which makes perfect sense, but it doesn't quite put the spotlight on the rhythmic resource on which this poetry (so much) depends: speech, and the fact that in English the syllables that make up words are either stressed or unstressed. This is too clumsy a distinction, in my opinion, and I prefer *strong* or *weak* syllables, because in this scheme the pulse never disappears. Rhythm in speech (and poetry) is the interplay between strong and weak syllables. Let's jump over to music for a moment. Generally, the pulse is broken down into twos or threes, with larger units being composed of groups of these two. One is certainly possible, though it's typically subdivided—again in twos or threes. Also, certain beats are usually strong, such as beat one in a unit of three and beats one and three in a unit of four (n.b.: part of what makes American music so distinctive is that beats two and four are strong). What does this have to do with words? Well, while English has plenty of monosyllabic words, it also has plenty of polysyllabic words, and here are one of each: "Strawberry Blond". I would like to apply some musical thinking to get at what's going on here rhythmically. Let's take "Strawberry". Here's how it's accented: "Straw-ber-ry". Interestingly, each syllable is roughly equivalent in length. If you don't believe me, try fitting *strawberry* into a foot of dactylic hexameter (long-short-short, with two short = one long). It sounds great (as if a baseball announcer was pronouncing Darryl Strawberry's name with a flourish), but it's not how the word is ordinarily pronounced. No, *straw-ber-ry* is a rhythmic unit of three beats, and as proof I offer the Beatles' song "Strawberry Fields Forever." The line "strawberry fields forever" actually marks the song's brief use of quarter-note triplets (triplet = three beats). As for "Blond", its appearance following the two weak-stress syllables ("ber-ry") fits perfectly, since as I mentioned earlier beat one in a unit of three gets the stress: "Straw-ber-ry Blond"—one-two-three-one.

The point here is not to reduce speech to music. I simply want to point out where in part the rhythm in speech is located, and though it may be irregular (or variable, as Williams put it), its presence in modern American poetry doesn't just come out of thin air.

DUNCAN McNAUGHTON

Selon Becht

Clabbart comes out of the men's with a case
of crabs. Cold in there. Completely off the
subject. You want them cracked, he smiles, or you
want to eat them whole? To the triplets at
the bar. Maureen, Colleen and Eileen. The
Devlin Sisters. Chilly conversation.

What causes you, Mo asks. What's happening
here is arriving at the same time its
moment is. Once, he says. Like ice.

Christmas Morning on the Coast

You're not kidding there's a story behind that.
George has the sniffles. The best I can do:
imagine a word and its worlds. Harlem,
though ordinarily, because of the
cold weather, you don't associate this
with sentimentality, had two *a*'s.

At supper the young Croatian skin of
the woman seated to my left, I can't
keep my eyes from her complexion, from her
face, her neck, her arms, everse translucence,
Illyrian I would say, tribal in
a way back glacial way, when gods were us
before we devolved. Prior to all this.
Only she hasn't. Of an age before;
another distance too. Each of us is
someone else. Va bene. Crystal eyes.

Dry east wind, doves aloft the rooftops, mild
bright air, pure blue sky. Southwest, beyond the
Moorish tiles of Mission High's tall dome, one
quiet little airplane, heading south. To
summarize, the teeth I like most these days
are those in the smile of Raoul Coutard.

Minutes, Rain, Madame Ng

We give him very high marks, the bus is
late again, for equanimity, marks
among the highest we've ever conferred
in a category we have seldom
awarded any marks at all, as most,
the new bus stop shelters are leaking rain,
nominees are so bedeviled by their
mirrored reflections that, hats on or off,
merit fails, umbrellas, no umbrellas,
to find its reason; the faithful are drenched.
We agreed that it had been a mistake to
include Derek Jeter in the final
comparison, as the benefits of
miscegenation, criminality
with bohemianism, hitherto
politically usable, have been
outlived. Poetry has moved on to
the scales of dispossession. We forget,
do both Leviathan and Moloch wear
an armor made of those? Gutters flooded.

Being as it mayn't be otherwise,
today we drove behind a license plate
which read WM BLAKE. Generic
Japanese beige, trunk Gorilla-taped shut.
No wonder Superman can't find his cape.

Well, what's needed, neopluvialish,
in a trustworthy boat, reliable
map such as the night sky, hunter/farmer
skills, sundries i.e., sharpened sundering
implements, and a crew consisting of
persons with very high marks awarded
for equanimity, private, public

Getting there, getting back, customary
debriefing, vessel's prow deciphered, then
off to bed to be read to before sleep
by Bobby Brown.

JASON MORRIS

Homemade Triple Sevens

for Bill Berkson

Light freight
for the scenic route
then the plunge
back into enigma

      liberally living amid books
confirming the status of
terminus as a Janus word—terminal to terminal, bright
      gate

Sounds heard in songs lead to
big neatly spattered canvases,
some parking lots a few
palm trees form a vault above

    & the double-sided
    chrome adhesive
    poems are, or more

conversation, French bread, the
live oaks cats track tanagers around

bearing coincidental resemblance
to homemade Boeings red as cardinals,
works that sped through nighttime drizzle

    "all saints on deck"

    there is no
    terminal

angling headlong up bright
rain then post-

      cloud light

MEL NICHOLS

Deep Fun: Hymns of St. Bridget, by Bill Berkson and Frank O'Hara

Hymns of St. Bridget begins simply enough in October 1960 as the first col-
laboration between Bill Berkson and Frank O'Hara—from there it multiplies
energetically into an ongoing exchange between Berkson and O'Hara that
includes the FYI poems "The Letters of Angelicus and Fidelio" and "Marcia:
An Unfinished Novel." The synergistic impact of this poetic alliance extends
beyond the literal collaborations and can be seen, for example, in the many
poems by O'Hara referencing Berkson between 1960 and 1962: "For the
Chinese New Year & for Bill Berkson," "Bill's Burnoose," "Biotherm (for Bill
Berkson)," and others. Beyond "Biotherm"—a long poem that begins as a
sort of pseudo-meditation on a skin cream—O'Hara further engages the
chatty style explored in *Hymns* through a series of dialogues with television
shows and films. "The Jade Madonna" (1964) has, for instance, the ambi-
ance of the poet in collaboration with an old Western movie:

> I'll give him two more   and if he don't think of
> days
> a way to get Wyatt Earp out of here
> by then
>
>   I'm going to
>   plant some
>   corpses.

And then:

> I got $820. $820? Yeah dollars. I kind of like having property.
>
> Possession is better
> than   a ranch. That's why I collect
> all these things that have nothing
> to do
>   with cows
>   with dollars or with the great open
>   range.

                                    Smell that?
    that's my cows thinking about my money.
                                    (*Collected Poems* 484–85)

"Fantasy"—dedicated to the health of Allen Ginsberg and wrapped
around scenes from the 1943 World War II film *Northern Pursuit*—is also
O'Hara in high filmic/conversational mode:

The main thing is to tell a
story.   It is almost

very important. Imagine
                        throwing away the avalanche
so early in the movie. I am the only
spy left
in Canada,
            but just because I'm alone in the
snow doesn't necessarily mean I'm a Nazi.
                            Let's see,
two aspirins a vitamin C tablet and some
baking soda should do the trick, that's
practically an
                            Alka
Seltzer. Allen come out of the bathroom
                            and take it [. . .

. . .] Allen, are you feeling any better? Yes, I'm
crazy about Helmut Dantine
                but I'm glad that Canada will remain
free. Just free, that's all, never argue with the movies.   (488)

   Lytle Shaw, in his essay "Gesture in 1960," provides yet another portrait
of O'Hara composing through the ludic play of conversation in his dis-
cussion of O'Hara's 1960 collaboration with the painter Norman Bluhm,
Poem-Paintings. Bluhm emphasizes the "spontaneous and intersocial as-
pects of working on all the tacked up Poem-Paintings at once" (40) while
hanging out in the studio and listening to music. As with the Berkson-
O'Hara collaborations, Bluhm characterizes his work with O'Hara as

"instantaneous, like a conversation between friends" (40). In an interview Bluhm notes that all the pieces in the collaboration "came out of some hilarious relationship with people we knew, out of a particular situation" (qtd. in Shaw 38). Does the analogy of gesture—as used in painting—work when applied to writing? Can it apply to the role of conversation in the work? Berkson, in a recent interview, explains the intersection of conversation, gesture, and writing when he describes gesture as linking the space of a poem and the breath, perhaps like Olson or Kyger or Ginsberg. And he points to the physical presence of the line as a poem is composed, "the line moving through space-time" (Berkson interview).

"What is the role of humor?" I asked Bill Berkson over the phone. The way he paused, it sounded like maybe he thought it was a bad question. "The role . . . of humor . . . ," he said slowly, ". . . is . . . to have . . . fun." He repeated it with no hesitation: "The role of humor is to have fun. To keep things rolling. It's the only way to do collaboration. To roll it. Most of it is having fun—fun between friends." Berkson notes that "in the collaborations there is a sense of having fun, of humor—that is the way to do it . . . Allen Ginsberg talked about deep gossip—so why not deep humor? I'm sure there are deep, lyric moments in the collaboration. But one can also have deep humor."

The story of how the collaboration *Hymns of St. Bridget* got rolling can be found in the notes of the Owl Press publication of the book (83). Berkson and O'Hara were walking along First Avenue and noticed the crooked steeple on a church—which I imagine was likened to a limp phallus—and they laughed about it. Berkson went home, still thinking about the drooping steeple of St. Bridget's Church, and wrote "Hymn to St. Bridget's Steeple" in what he calls "a sort of poor imitation of O'Hara"(Berkson interview). "It is to you, bending limp and ridiculous, on Ninth / Street, that I turn" (13) begins the first poem of *Hymns of St. Bridget*, a conversational-rhetorical direct address Berkson considers his imitation of the high O'Hara or Ginsberg mode. "I showed it to Frank and he said, 'Why don't we do a series of these?'"

When Berkson came to O'Hara with the poem he had just written, it had not occurred to him to make the work into a collaboration. The young Berkson had done just one collaboration, with Kenward Elmslie, which was later published in the Summer 1961 collaboration issue of *Locus Solus*, edited by Kenneth Koch. *Hymns* proceeded, at O'Hara's urging, with the next poem in the series, "St. Bridget's Neighborhood":

St. Bridget I wish you would wake up and tend my bumper
It's cracked it is like the thought

I had of you when I cut myself shaving "O steeple
why don't you help me as you helped the Missouri islanders?"   (15)

The two poets—O'Hara in his mid-thirties and Berkson in his twenties
—wrote *Hymns* my-turn-your-turn style at a single typewriter:

> The
> afternoon is leaning toward drinks I am
> getting
>
> myself one now though I shouldn't
>   Would
> you like one, heaviness of the compost
> thresh-
>
> hold? No, I want the plants to have
> it, for they have died
>
>   ("St. Bridget's Neighborhood" 14)

At this point in the story, I should offer an explanation about the subject of *Hymns of St. Bridget* in the context of a symposium of books published in 1960—for *Hymns* was not published until 1974, by Adventures in Poetry. In fact, only two of the poems from the collaboration were ever published during O'Hara's lifetime, in the May/June 1962 issue of *Evergreen Review* ("Hymn to St. Bridget's Steeple" and "Us Looking Up to St. Bridget"). 1960 was, however, the beginning of this significant poetic dialogue between Berkson and O'Hara. *Hymns of St. Bridget* launched a flurry of collaboration, beginning aptly with the two poets walking along First Avenue and laughing.

By 1960, O'Hara had well established his "I Do This and I Do That" style and so came to the collaboration with these gestures in hand—and Berkson notes that of course he was heavily influenced by O'Hara's work at that time. Berkson himself was increasingly working with open field pieces, as evidenced by poems dating from 1959 to 1961 and published in *All You Want* (1966):

          my hat
          your . . . the crumplings of an
          evening put forward as ice was

               ah trolley!
          the except
               our still-life yearnings allow tunes
               to the far suburbs
                    (from "Four Great Songs," *Portrait and Dream* 47)

If ludic play is significant throughout the collaborations between O'Hara
and Berkson, then it is perhaps also an important contributor to the
so-called third voice of collaboration as well. O'Hara's work increasingly
moves from painterly to filmic, and the poems become increasingly
untamed and open as they accumulate. "I think Frank was very excited
by this," says Berkson, "and on his own he began to write things that were
wilder and wilder, leading up to 'Biotherm.'"

     troika   And back at the organ the angel was able to play
     a great single green tree for the opening of the new bank
     Caracallo   it was
     the loin   the last opening of a bank anywhere because the
     angel's wings sloth   got clipped in the swimming pool
     it   ate   well   and   had   glorious   nightmares
               days she
               hated   it "Satan, hélas? c'est vous?" April
               had rushed into May while
                              she was reading Hollywood Babylon

     and now the trees wore evil fringes where buzzards
                              roosted covered with old
                              prayer beads

          An awning flapped.
          ("St. Bridget's Hymn to Philip Guston" 29–30)

134

WORKS CITED

Berkson, Bill. *Portrait and Dream: New and Selected Poems*. Minneapolis: Coffee House Press, 2009.

———. Interview with Mel Nichols. 27 November 2010.

Berkson, Bill, and Frank O'Hara. *Hymns of St. Bridget*. New York: Adventures in Poetry, 1974.

———. *Hymns of St. Bridget & Other Writings*. Woodacre, CA: Owl Press, 2001.

O'Hara, Frank. *The Collected Poems of Frank O'Hara*. New York: Alfred A. Knopf, 1979.

Shaw, Lytle. "Gesture in 1960: Toward Literal Solutions." *Frank O'Hara Now*. Eds. Robert Hampton and Will Montgomery. Liverpool: Liverpool University Press, 2010.

ALICE NOTLEY

All of That Street

for Bill Berkson

Rivers unwind in a purloined dreaming, black and the colors of the novitiate:
roomful of steins red, blue, yellow, green, & white; the secrets of the stars.
I have one, and so do you; the others are too self-absorbed. That is, a credit
    card,
your mother's. For she was great—Corinne was too, explicitly take care of
and especially you who are vested—it's tan—in a striking decency, mauve
    shirt,
bearded (later). Why, any topic, as long as you like; it's raining art or mattering
and we don't ever sign off. I remember Vera Ralston, in a sarong or culotte;
I remember the puzzled magician—not a pigeon, but a light, emerged;
under the big sky everyone's heavenly dusk oh you occasion to whistle (I
can't). Sorrow a sand dollar, with a formal shape caught forever in its dna—
who's listening? to the sung woe or wu. I was stunned, but this isn't about me
babe are suddenly there, the humor, the fresh, the Rose. It is a pasta dish
made with spaghettini, sage, parmesan, a drop of milk, and pepper—no
    salt:
though you are a courageous captain, unsanctimonious. By your dreamy
    guest.

KEVIN OPSTEDAL

Drawn Blank

for Pope Benedict XI & Bill Berkson

A seagull wheels & pivots in the sky

describing the arc of a compass

a prayer-wheel windchime

racking up the zeroes

a roundelay

a self-devouring hula hoop

        rolling downhill?

I don't know, Bill, but I'm sure of

two or three things

    each of which are water soluble

        like a bubble in a mile of milk

any minute now

      doo-wah-ditty-dum

ditty-doom

& standing outside the Del Taco in Ventura

on Chinese New Year

                          in the rain
        Giotto dips his brush in red

        paint

                    & in one continuous stroke

        draws a perfect circle

RON PADGETT

Birgitte Hohlenberg

for Bill

I do not know who Birgitte Hohlenberg was
or why C. A. Jensen painted her portrait, in 1826,
but I'm glad he did, because then I could see it
in the Statens Museum for Kunst in Copenhagen
and buy a postcard of it and send it to my wife:
"Isn't she beautiful?" She being
Birgitte Hohlenberg *and* the painting of her.
I don't know which of them I love more.
Both are bright, calm, and sweet—
she had a way with beauty. You see it
in the brown satin dress with fluffy sleeves
and big white collar edged in lace, the hat
a light white puff around her head
and neatly tied beneath the chin,
her curly chestnut hair an echo
of the ribbon curling around the brim
and returning over the shoulders
to a loose knot at the collarbone,
her slender neck rising to a face whose high color elevates
how interested she is to be sitting there
looking straight at you without the slightest hint of carnality.
Just being in her presence would be enough
for me, now, at my age.
When did I send this card? August 15,
2001. That long ago. Before the Towers came down—
before a lot of things came down. But she
has stayed up, on my wife's dresser. How
she died I don't know, or at what age.
C. A. Jensen lived to 78, a long life
back then. Good for him.
I hope he was as happy
as he makes me every time I see his picture.
I think you should see it too.

I have had the great opportunity to publish not just one poetry book by
Bill Berkson (*Serenade*, in 2000, with a cover painting by Joe Brainard), but
two (*Fugue State*, in 2001, with a cover painting by Yvonne Jacquette). Bill's
poems insisted themselves on me, and made me feel like a winner. I got
to present the work of a poet I much admire. I won the triple crown: as a
reader, editor, and publisher. Bill, thank you for writing all that you do.

Two poems for Bill Berkson:

Upbringing

Millions stride in Manhattan. They walk the pavement with their tons of feet.
Shoe to shoe they flow their way uptown, downtown, east and west. Born at

the Flower Fifth Avenue Hospital, I grew up on East End Avenue. I recall:
The Giants, The Dodgers (not to mention the New York Yankees) on the radio.

My team: The Red Sox. Art on our walls: Rivers, Hartigan, Goodnough
Grooms, Frankenthaler, Blaine. Fairfield Porter as well . . . Bomb shelters

Curb Your Dog signs, Horn & Hardart, Ethel Merman and Maria Tallchief,
the lure of Times Square and the Village. Tibor de Nagy, Bobby Wagner

August my barber on Lexington, Vitalis, Buckley. Knickerbocker Greys,
    deRham's,
St. James Church, Sunday at Prexy's (the hamburger with the college
    education).

And Dad, Deb, Me:
Such a threesome.

To The Writers

Writers I have
read. Writers
I have known

Poets who play
with my mind

To those I've taken
and had the great
chance to publish

I doff my hat to you

BOB PERELMAN

Early Bill: Two Postcards

1: BILL LIKES *WOW*

After I gave Bill *Braille*, I heard he liked one of the words from one of the pieces: *Wow*, from "Atlantis," the improvisation where I had discovered, like puberty, one-word sentences—you could say that Bill liked one of the sentences from the piece.

It was great that Bill liked *Wow*. But then, how particular was he being? Could you generalize out to the rest of the book? even the rest of the improvisation? Or was it just *Wow*?

Some years later, Bill quoted it to me in a note, which made it kind of a password. Pre-linguistic enthusiasm with punctuation serving as con-sciousness: *Wow*.

When I was assembling the "Talks" issue of *Hills* in 1980, I put Bill's talk first. It had the appropriate title: "Talk" seemed the right way for "Talks" to begin.

Plus, it contained a long letter from Frank O'Hara to Bill, and O'Hara seemed a great anti-ancestor to preside over the issue in general. The letter lay athwart a number of agendas. It was a passionate disquisition on the possibility, in music, of "the unplanned image"—or rather the impossibility, since the unplanned image was something O'Hara had never "heard with his ears." No composer, not Mozart, not Cage, Boulez, Stockhausen, no one had ever managed it. But music seemed something that O'Hara had heard, with his ears and with his mind, quite clearly. He had no patience for "intellectual joiners who never listen anyway" or for generalizing "avant-gardists" who are merely boosting "the forward-marching army of themselves."

Perhaps the impossibility of the unplanned image came from O'Hara's sense of composition as "a basically Platonic operation, with the most bizarre sentimental preoccupations acting as both inspiration and response-from-the-auditors, executed under an appalling dictatorship of mechanical manipulations and exactitudes which the composer must either use for his own purposes or circumvent."

Bill Berkson 1961; photo by Kenward Elmslie

Bill read out the letter, and said nothing to contradict it. In fact, he defended it against some avant-garde skepticism. But Bill's talk proper was about talk and extolled the middle voice. It was completely distinct from the Niagara of tone-painting he had just read. The juxtaposition was so clean and unremarked that it could have as easily been in the service of synthesis as of difference.

The "Talks" issue came out. I felt rather proud as I handed a copy to Bill. It seemed imposingly thick (in those homegrown days), and Francie's cover was great (five schematic "ears" collaged into an audience—making the point that the ear was a speech organ). The past was over: here are the "Talks." Bill thanked me and opened to a page of the transcribed conversation in "Talk." He read for a second. "Hemmingway?" he said, genuinely amuse

d. It was an excellent typo.

SIMON PETTET

Satori

for Bill

Ignatz throws his brick
and the glorious world is revealed
for what it is—glorious.
Ignatz throws his brick
and the heavens are opened.
Ignatz throws his brick and
The combined forces of a
Unit of weight, in velocity,
Approximately x pounds,
heat-seeks its target.
I'm coming to you, sir, officer,
I'm coming to you as a zephyr,
Sans disturbance.
I expect little stars to appear
All around your head.

I expect you to be bemused
but finally realize

Bill Berkson schooled my partner, Colter Jacobsen, at the San Francisco Art Institute. And he taught him something profound. Colter was new to San Francisco and fascinated, as many are, with the city's radical past. But that wasn't quite enough for Bill, who urged Colter to "find his own '6os," or something to that effect. I've heard the story from Colter several times, so I know it made an impression on him.

Bill, who has not only seen but *been* enough of history to rest comfortably on his laurels, should he so choose, instead throws himself wholly into the present. He is ubiquitous at openings, lectures, screenings, readings and as engaged with the work of young artists and poets as he is with the works of established masters. Bill's "own '6os" is the timeless, life-affirming, community-shaping energy of art.

I use the term *art* broadly, of course, as Bill's primary métier and his personal creative outlet is words. Poems and essays, sure, but also his everyday speech. Even when he speaks informally, you can hear in the cadence of his voice the measure of his thoughts and the heart of his meaning.

Bill himself came up during the Golden Age of New York culture, before creativity in that town became hopelessly commodified and the disciplines isolated like so many independent industrial sectors. I'm sure we owe not a little of our own remarkable cosmopolitanism to the living example of his broad-minded erudition and catholic enthusiasms.

Colter is only one of dozens (hundreds, probably) whom Bill has alerted to the responsibility to live largely, love widely, and make history their own. But Colter is the one I get to enjoy the most, so thanks, Bill, your pedagogy is much appreciated . . . by us both.

KIT ROBINSON

My Dream a Drink with Bill Berkson

Dream of a big collaborative painting with Bill Berkson. Bill is playing fast and loose with the materials, combining word and image willy-nilly—anything goes. Now black paint on white canvas, now orange magic marker on stainless steel. I cover an area with scribbled content, unsure of myself but eager to engage. Connie is standing about on the periphery, commenting on the action, providing context. I take the finished product—is it—on my shoulders, in fact a whole stack of them, angle through a wide doorway and head upstairs. The work is to be hung in the bedroom. Great excitement and nervy exuberance all around.

I first met Bill at Yale in 1969. He had come to teach a weekly workshop at Ezra Stiles College, and I was to interview him for the student-run *New Journal.* When asked his opinion of a then-popular poet, I've forgotten whom (John Berryman?), Bill said he was too much under the influence of Yeats and Eliot. Then he said something about poetry and happiness, that there was no reason why the poet couldn't also be the happiest of people, or words to that effect, that appealed to me. As against the shopworn angst of the presiding pantheon, Lowell et al., it was a decidedly unfashionable opinion and one that fit my determination to pull myself out of the dark shallows of existential dread.

Breakfast with Bill at the Plaza Hotel in Milwaukee, April 2009. He gives me a copy of *Missing*, a gorgeous color-print edition of a book of student collages from New Rochelle High School. On each page, a fragment of Bill's poems "Missing" and "Missing (2)" above an amazing collage by a student. The verse fragments are composed of wicked smart throwaway lines like "The workers' thought-process exposes the shark face of nations beneath an elevator shaft"; "Veteran ding-a-lings applaud Earth's curfew from Nirvana Lodge"; "The swamp's remembrance is a human ramp"; and "What is that mothball / doing in the strawberries?" I wonder at the complexity of this material within the context of the suburban high school classroom. Yet it obviously worked. The collages are wild, witty, and passionate statements about sex, class, art, politics, art, death, and country. Clearly, there has been a total engagement here in terms that allow for maximum freedom of expression. How does he do it!?

Early Bill, 1959–1961. When he was twenty, twenty-one, twenty-two years old, Bill wrote these incredibly sophisticated New York poems. He was evidently getting some very positive feedback, and it seems to have given him confidence to last a lifetime. The very first poem in his *Selected*, "October," is a nifty Stevensesque conceit. Then the ice breaks. "History" owes more to "Europe" than to subsequent Ashbery. It is all broken up. Yet held together by what? Or should I say, by whom? "Primitive American sophisticate."

Sometime in the late '70s, Bill did a collaboration with Barrett Watten. Working in prose, the two wrote alternate paragraphs and read the completed piece someplace, I can't remember where, the Grand Piano? Later each published his own passages as a separate work. Barry's became "Plasma," the lead piece in his seminal 1979 Tuumba chapbook *Plasma / Paralleles / "X."* Bill's became "Loralei," if I am not mistaken. BW: "A paradox is eaten by the space around it." BB: "One of the worst sins Dante could think of was to sulk in the sunlight. Those who did he assigned the eternal punishment of wallowing in mud." BW: "I'll repeat what I said." BB: "When I met ___, I really had the impression of seeing a saint. My first impulse was to put my head on his shoulder to get protection, which I didn't do." BW: "To make a city into a season is to wear sunglasses inside a volcano." BB: "A corner becomes the top (loaded dice?), and the space inside is fantastic, however dim." BW: "He never forgets his dreams." BB: "Amid hordes of after-dinner sitters in 'pumps,' D. H. Lawrence gets up and throws a wet fish on the table."

My parents were visiting from Cincinnati. We went to a party at Lynn O'Hare and Bill's place in Bolinas. It was a beautiful sunny summer day. Joanne and Donald must have been there. Bill was charming as always. I was happy. This was in the '80s.

The second half of my prose sequence "Entropica" first appeared in Bill's *Big Sky* magazine, issue 10, 1976. I was so proud for it to be included. I'd proofread several issues of *Big Sky* along with Barrett Watten, who was doing the typesetting. That was when I learned to read aloud for speed, a skill I later utilized as a legal proofreader at Brobeck, Phleger & Harrison. I remember one time early on with Bill and Lynn at Barry's apartment on 22nd Street near Guerrero. Lynn said something, something, Daddy . . . then interrupted herself: "Here I am thirty years old, and I'm still calling my father Daddy!" To me, Lynn and Bill seemed incalculably older and *très plus soigner*.

BB as suave young gentleman, Greta Garbo's "ice cream man," man about town, confidant of Bianca Jagger. His good looks and courtly manners invite suspicions of superficiality that are instantly dispelled by his resolute attention to surfaces of all kinds—surfaces of art, life, and thought. So the princely stuff kind of falls away. But then there it is again, after all this time, a sweetness, a kind of grace or ease, that seems entirely ethical in its generous, open disposition—available, curious, and unpretentious.

I remember Bill in 1963 reading his poems one evening at the Kornblee Gallery on the Upper East Side. In his twenties, he was both strikingly handsome and a bit daunting. It was as if he wasn't certain that the audience would take him exactly as he wanted and wasn't about to surrender any ground. In retrospect, one might surmise that he hadn't set out on the easiest path, and this self-possession, if not necessarily welcoming, was a measure of his commitment.

In five years' time, given the solvent of the rising tide of the second generation of the New York School of poets, I would be a beneficiary of his casual, sixties-style generosity—Gailyn and I stayed in his Village apartment for several nights when he was out of town—but without feeling that I knew him very well. In fact, it was mostly from others that I learned about Bill: that he responded very warmly to the poetry of my friend Jenni Caldwell, for instance, when others hadn't been interested. Edwin Denby, the nearest thing to a father figure in our group, told me admiringly that while Bill was heterosexual he wouldn't hesitate to hug and kiss his friend Frank O'Hara when they met in public.

As the seventies began, he left New York, and had established a home in Bolinas when Gailyn and I arrived there in 1972. We eventually became nearby neighbors on the mesa, and it was now that I got to know him better in a variety of contexts: as the editor of his magazine *Big Sky* and (with Joe LeSueur) of the festschrift *Homage to Frank O'Hara*, as a fellow member of the Bolinas social round, and as a friend and supporter of a wide spectrum of young writers, from his New York pal Jim Carroll to the poets John Thorpe and Jim Gustafson, among others, published by him in his Big Sky book series. In addition, as a couple Gailyn and I shared the experience of raising young children with Bill and his then-wife Lynn O'Hare.

With space at a premium in their house on Fern Road, he converted the garage into an office, and uniquely among Bolinas poets seemed to keep office hours. Of Frank O'Hara he remarked one day: "He was one of the last generation so well educated that they knew about everything." He was then making his way through *The Divine Comedy*, as I remember. "There's this thing of having *too* many ideas, you know?" he said on another day. Carefully and steadily, he was writing both his art criticism and his poems.

In short, without making anything of it, he was a sturdy exemplar of the kind of life possible for us. When he and Lynn went east one year, he lent us a small Philip Guston painting, something one wouldn't have conceived of asking him to do. With the Guston in our house, on a daily basis we all breathed in what felt like an aesthetic wonder. One afternoon a year or so later, Bill invited us to a small gathering at the center of which stood Guston himself, with a demeanor that seemed to replicate the painting. It was like standing next to an upright river.

I all but lost touch with Bill when we left Bolinas in 1984 for several years on the East Coast before settling again in California, this time Southern California. In recent years I heard that he was ill, and then that he had successfully undergone a lung transplant operation. When another friend of mine was contemplating the same operation, I got in touch again, and Bill responded quickly with support and advocacy.

More recently, in a review of a book of his poems in the Trinity School alumni magazine—at different times we'd each attended Trinity—I read his poem about Roy Eldridge, which somehow perfectly captures a resonant trumpet tone, and realized he was at the top of his form after well-nigh half a century.

Gailyn and I recently joined Bill and Connie to see the Gorky show at the Museum of Contemporary Art in Los Angeles, and I saw again my old friend: curious, gentle, generous, and astute as ever—a gift of the years I recognized now with simple pleasure.

CEDAR SIGO

Marble Harbor

for Bill Berkson

The apartment feels like newspaper
headquarters—
orange light facing off the brick. It's
Clark Kent coming into work, we call him
the poet as he brings us the unknown, anything
that possesses him.

A second castle drawing (ink)
Engravings of Gainsbourg, abacus, earplugs, empty spools
Slivers, A gold mine outside a mansion under a palm tree. . . .

Lust is the main distraction I find, it
seems to interrupt
the flow. December the 21st colored by and by
It's like that
in the crawlspace, lines are more ribbon
than wood.

One does see the sphinx
but the sphinx stands

for a secret (gods
or circulating forces) I never knew anyone
with a profundity of tact that came close.

We all know
we are just playing house.
O blessed plain O pointed
chasm. New Feudalism.

Distillation of a night
the poets would pay for . . . amish apple butter and snow

we kept for you in our freezer.
Sweeping my unruly works
into a book, laid side by side, I just see dollar signs.
A love whose burning light shall warm the winter night, that's all.

ROD SMITH

Poem Composed of Lines from Poems by Bill Berkson

for Bill Berkson

O rare-at-night felicity
A favorite plant has reproduced itself

Thus has prehistory entered your life

The Stork Club is closed.

more violins ahead

He was dashing, with his heroic profile as sharp as the prow of a boat, and seemed in the early days to be moving at a speed that generated a little wind or wake, but even his smile was quick, and he always slowed down enough to say hello, and once, I remember, whirl me around the line waiting to get in to a San Francisco Art Institute lecture hall event as though we were instead at a grand evening ball. Maybe for a moment we were. I was so young I thought of people older than me as "grown-ups" when I first met Bill Berkson sometime in the mid-1980s or earlier, though how I met this grown-up and where I don't know: I got to know him by degrees, and never well, but well enough to be grateful for specific kindnesses and for a space of integrity and engagement he carves out by living his life as he did and does. I asked him to write the introduction to my first book, *Secret Exhibition*, which was about the visual artists who were part of Beat culture on the West Coast, because I thought Bill, who had himself been a poet among painters and who'd lived through some roughly parallel things on the East, might be able to situate this story for Easterners and general readers. He explained the context and the issues graciously—grace might be his signature virtue—and I still remember two things from that essay often. One is his description of coming to San Francisco in the summer of 1958, an undergraduate officially looking for a newspaper job and unofficially looking for poets in the hangouts of North Beach. He reports, the way a birder reports an osprey or a green heron, that he saw Jack Spicer "huddled alone in the fog" on the now-vanished traffic island at Columbus and Broadway. The other is the epigraph from Myrna Loy, "The common tragedy is to have suffered without having 'appeared.'" Bill has appeared on many scenes and stages, gracefully, moving through them and on to others, though he's been docked in the Bay Area for forty years now, and I'm still grateful.

Idea men—and idea women—are a dime a dozen these days. The art
academies and art magazines are overrun with them. In seminar rooms,
in galleries, and at parties, they crowd each other, elbows out and tongues
a-wagging. Their predicament—and I feel for them in their desper-
ate desire to astonish themselves and one another—reminds me of an
exchange between Mallarmé and Degas. The two were friends and mutual
fans, and as sometimes happens in such circumstances, one man's vocation
became the other's avocation—his "violon d'Ingres." So it was that Degas
took to writing sonnets. Frustrated in his efforts, he complained to his
mentor Mallarmé that he was at a loss as how to proceed because he lacked
ideas. To which Mallarmé responded, "But my dear Edgar, sonnets are
made of words, not ideas."

A poet first and foremost, Bill Berkson knows this better than anyone
currently engaged in the honorable though much maligned craft of art
criticism. That awareness of the generative promise and power of words
gives him the capacity and confidence to write about art of all kinds and
all periods, from the Renaissance to the latest Chelsea shows, from paint-
erly painters in the grand tradition like Alex Katz to new media magi
like Bruce Nauman, from inspired sensualists to, well, idea men. That he
follows his own intuition in choosing his subject without deference to the
logic of prevailing discourses is a sign of his intellectual rigor rather than
of an absence of it. Good minds never scorn the things to which they are
attracted. Instead they go to work on them in order to get to the bottom of
that attraction, in order to extract the full measure of experience they have
to offer. And good writers deliver that experience to others, not least the
experience of figuring out how one became involved in an image or object,
especially if it is of the sort that one initially doubts or was puzzled by.

By that and every other definition, Bill is an exceptional writer of admi-
rably catholic taste, an always reliable go-to man for readers who crave
freshness of eye, ear, and mind, a phrasemaker of such natural talent he
dignifies that usually disparaging term, lending it the positive artisanal
connotations of blacksmith, wheelwright, cabinetmaker. Art suggests
words, words suggest ideas, ideas shed light back on art; that is the fertile

cycle that engenders Bill's criticism, it being a branch of his primary métier, poetry. Bill has never had Degas's problem, but he chose to write about art on the side rather than fashion as Mallarmé did. However, Mallarmé wrote beautifully about dresses because he knew where writing comes from, and had Bill decided to tackle the runways rather than the galleries, we'd still read him. Lucky for us, though, he didn't. As a result, we have his insights into the dynamics of the visual as well as the verbal. If only he'd tell the tale of how he has done it all and how he has lived a life so well balanced between his two great passions. May Berkson the memoir writer introduce himself to us next.

DAVID LEVI STRAUSS

Sweet Singer Strikes Again

Recently, I was going through the chronology for the catalogue of the 2003–04 Philip Guston retrospective at the Modern Art Museum of Fort Worth, Texas, and under the heading "1962" I found the line, "Begins friendship with poet Bill Berkson." Two things occurred to me. First, how many friends would merit an entry like that? And second, this line could actually appear in many artists' and writers' chronologies, and if you plotted a graph of these myriad beginnings and continuances, you would come up with a compelling map of an alternative history of American art and poetry over the last half century.

In my personal chronology, that line would appear under the heading "1981," when I was a twenty-eight-year-old "apprentice lyric poet" in San Francisco, studying in the poetics program at New College with Robert Duncan, Michael Palmer, Diane di Prima, David Meltzer, Duncan McNaughton, and other poets. That August, I wrote to Bill to invite him to read in a series that Aaron Shurin and I were organizing at a small gallery/theater south of Market called 544 Natoma. Bill immediately replied, graciously accepting my invitation, and our conversation began. It continued for some time, including a class I took from Bill in the poetics program titled "Vernacular Poetics" that was billed as "an emergency course in common sense to deal with the present 'splendid state of confusion' re: poetic intentions and requirements, assuming most of the usual terms . . . are questionable, and that, poem by poem, such poetic/esthetic definition and pronouncement is up for grabs." Our conversation abated when I moved to New York in 1993. It was thankfully renewed in 2006, when I interviewed Bill for the *Brooklyn Rail* and later invited him to appear in my lecture series at the School of Visual Arts, where I had just been appointed chair of the graduate program in art criticism & writing.

Since then, Bill's art writing has become prominent in our curriculum at SVA, as an example of what is possible in the form. In the *Rail* interview, Bill said:

> If art is a form of social behavior—and I can't imagine it being taken as anything else—it exists as a sort of conversation: you make some-

thing and pass it along, across the room, so to speak. You show it. The addressee may be specific or a phantasmagoria.

One of the things I've always appreciated about Bill's approach to writing about art, in addition to its sheer beauty, is his insistence on keeping his amateur status—remaining a true freelance. He ended a recent letter to me this way:

> Best we fumble along, "irrelevant" belles-lettrists that we are . . .
> Poetry, as all the art people would tell you, is beside the point. No cultural currency, they say, because the attendance figures are so low. Phooey. Poetry strikes back, gloriously beside the point.

In Bill's work, poetry strikes back with a particularly seductive subversion—gloriously beside the point, but all the more pointed, even so.

544 NATOMA

San Francisco CA 94103

19;VIII;81

Dear Bill Berkson,

    I lived with a painter for three years. Whenever
we discussed paintings, hers or someone else's, and it
got difficult, I would dust off my refrain: "I don't
know anything about painting! I'm an apprentice lyric
poet. I haven't the vaguest notion how painting even
occurs!" Then we'd talk some more.

    I picked up Rocky Ledge 8 for your "Travels With
Guston". I had asked you where I could find it after
the panel discussion at 80 Langton St. in July. This
talking with paintings rather than about them is a very
difficult business, and you make it look easy. I gave
up writing criticism of photography a few years ago
because I couldn't strike a balance. I kept finding
myself in the pulpit, tying neat little bows around
corpses.

    At one point in the class Michael Palmer taught
last Spring at New College, he moved through the
language of dancers talking about dance to show the
precision with which this language could be applied
to talking about poetry. Your snapshot of the "one
unifying principle" of the New York School cut through
reams of ponderous descriptions. And, "It's not like
God speaking, although you don't necessarily rule that
out either."

    I also reread your comments on "Talk" as a tall
order in the Hills anthology. The one thing I found
lacking in Perelman's series in general was poetry.
I made it a point to read the work of most of the
people I heard talk, but the series itself seemed to
tacitly consider the talking apart from the writing
and that never made sense to me. It was as if poetry
was being held at the door, denied entrance because of

Peter Hartman   621-2683
                                                        415 863-5425

lack of currency. Perhaps these are merely my pro-
jections. I was very young and very uncomfortable
in these rather doctrinaire proceedings.

Aaron Shurin and I are putting together a reading/
talk series at a small gallery/theater in San Francisco,
run by Peter Hartman. 544 Natoma has had a full sched-
ule of shows and performances for the last year, so
people know where it is.

Our intention is to provide a more in-depth ex-
posure to the works and words of select poets than is
offered in random, tandem readings. Each poet will
read his or her own work one Sunday evening, and give
a talk, performance, slide-lecture, etc. the next Sun-
day evening. All proceedings will be recorded on
audio or video tape, with copies available to the
readers. Payment will come from admission. The theatre
is set up for film/slide projection and theatrical
lighting. It seats over a hundred people.

Robert Duncan will begin the series with a "cabaret."
We're also asking Michael Palmer, Leslie Scalapino, Bob
Gluck, Kathy Acker, John Thorpe, Duncan McNaughton, Ron
Silliman, Judy Grahn, Anselm Hollo, and others.

If you are interested, please drop me a card at
the above address and we can discuss dates and other
specifics.

Sincerely,

David Levi Strauss

Box 389
Bolinas CA 94924

August 22, 1981

Dear David Levi Strauss,

Thanks for your nice
letter. It's so good to get feedback on anything
these days -- where, or to whom, does the writing,
not to mention any public talking, go? it's such
a funny, mostly unanswered, question. Poetry, as
you remark, is "held at the door," even by poets,
more often than not in this muddled present-time.
We could maybe talk about this some time. I suspect
that in some cases it is a matter of honesty.
Honestly, most of the poets I like to talk with,
and me too, now proceed in the most terrible
confusion about what the job is, and an obvious
desperation seems almost the only general rule.

Hm, that seems an odd lead into answering your
question about appearing at Natoma. But the series
does sound interesting, and yes, I'd like to take
part in it. Do you have a particular date in mind?
I think I would prefer later rather than earlier in
the season -- in any case, no sooner than November,
OK?

For the second evening, some kind of prepared talk
would probably be possible. But another flash I just
had: It might be fun to show some slides of paintings
& also one or two movies by Rudy Burckhardt & make
some kind of talking context for all that. Anyhow,
when the time comes, I'll mull it over.

Meanwhile, thanks again for letting me know your
thoughts on all those various scores.
When you see
Peter Hartman please remember me to him & say hello.

Best,

Bill Berkson

Note: These are books &/or works that will be sources for
the class. Ones marked with an asterisk (*) are required
reading. (Further required reading may be announced.)

*Longinus. ON THE SUBLIME.
Horace. Ars Poetica.
*Edmund Burke. PHILOSOPHICAL ENQUIRY INTO THE ORIGINS OF
        OUR IDEAS OF THE SUBLIME AND THE BEAUTIFUL.
Monk. The Sublime.

Ben Jonson. Timber.
Goethe. Conversations with Eckermann. ELECTIVE AFFINITIES.
*E.A. Poe. THE NARRATIVE OF A. GORDON PYM.
*Herman Melville. "After the Pleasure Party."

T.S. Eliot. Selected Essays.
        "The Wasteland" and "Marina."
Boris Pasternak. Safe Conduct.   *Barnett Newman monographs
Viktor Shklovsky. A Sentimental Journey.   have his essay on the Sub.
William Carlos Williams. Collected Later Poems.
        Imaginations.
        Many Loves.
*Edwin Denby. DANCERS, BUILDINGS AND PEOPLE IN THE STREETS.
        COLLECTED POEMS.

*Frank O'Hara. MEDITATIONS IN AN EMERGENCY.
        Standing Still and Walking in New York.
    *John Ashbery. THE TENNIS COURT OATH. 2 N.C. library
        The Vermont Notebook.

Fairfield Porter. ART IN ITS OWN TERMS.
Thomas B. Hess. WILLEM DE KOONING. (DeK's writings therein.)
PHILIP GUSTON (SFMA catalog).
*Robert Smithson. THE WRITINGS OF ROBERT SMITHSON.
Samuel Edgerton. The Renaissance Rediscovery of Linear Perspective.
Kenneth Clark. Piero Della Francesca.
Lawrence Gowing. Vermeer.
John Rewald. Cezanne.
Adrian Stokes. Image in Form.
Pierre Cabanne. Dialogues with Marcel Duchamp.

*Henry Green. Party Going.
        CONCLUDING.
        Pack My Bag.

*Dante Alighieri. LA VITA NUOVA.
        RIME(trans. Diehl, Princeton) ?

Thomas Wyatt. THE COMPLETE POEMS (Yale).
William Shakespeare. A Winter's Tale.
        *Sonnet XXIX.

Stéphane Mallarmé. Selected Poetry and Prose.
Francis Ponge. The Making of the Pré.
Denis Diderot. D'Alembert's Dream.

James Schuyler. FREELY ESPOUSING.
          The Morning of the Poem.
W.H. Auden. SELECTED POEMS (Vintage pb.)
Gertrude Stein. "Poetry and Grammar" in LECTURES IN AMERICA.
          STANZAS IN MEDITATION.
Rudy Burckhardt. Mobile Homes.

Other Sources:

Art News (1955-1966)
Art in America ('70s-'80s)

Laura Riding. Progress of Stories.
               Collected Poems.
Wallace Stevens. Collected Poems.
                 Opus Posthumous.
                 The Necessary Angel.
Bernadette Mayer. Midwinter Day.
                  Moving.
                  Studying Hunger.
Clark Coolidge. Own Face.
                American Ones.
Jack Kerouac. Visions of Cody.
A.B. Spellman. Four Lives in the Bebop Business.
A.N. Whitehead. Modes of Thought.
                The Aims of Education.
                Dialogues.
                Process and Reality.
Virgil Thomson. The Virgil Thomson Reader.
John McPhee. Oranges.
Robert Creeley. A Daybook.
Philip Whalen. On Bear's Head.
               Enough Said.
Alice Notley. Waltzing Matilda.
              Dr. Williams's Heiresses.
Ron Padgett. ToujoursL'Amour.
             "Cufflinks" in Triangles in the Afternoon.
John Thorpe. Exogeny.
Michael Brownstein. "Who Knows Where the Time Goes" in Brainstorms.
Kit Robinson. "A Sentimental Journey" in Hills 8.
D.G. Rossetti. Dante And His Circle.
Robert Duncan. The Sweetness and Greatness of Dante's Divine Comedy.
Osip Mandelstam. "Conversation About Dante" in Selected Essays.
Ted Greenwald. You Bet!
Berkson & Sandler, eds. Alex Katz.
John Wieners. Hotel Wentley Poems.
              Selected Poems.
Barnett Newman, writings in Hess catalog.
Tuchman, ed. The New York School (LA County Museum catalog).
Hobbs. ROBERT SMITHSON: SCULPTURE.
John Dryden. Versions of Vergil's Georgics.
John Leymarie. Balthus.
Jean-Luc Godard. Godard on Godard.

I.

Connie was slightly annoyed with Bill that a couple of his students had written that Bill's voice could become monotone during lectures. Bill shrugged apologetically but didn't refute the charges.

II.

"You can't ask your art to be more like you, because you don't know what that is. You can only ask it to be more like your life."

III.

A few of us accidentally found out that Bill would say "Yes" if you asked him for a studio visit. He is bottled lightning in a studio. "Okay, so this is a perfect painting" meant dead on arrival. "These colors are really terrible" and that was a good thing. Once in front of a flood of work he looked and looked in silence. He grabbed his coat and headed for the door. "Bear down."

IV.

I cast Bill in an experimental feature film I was making. He was supposed to bump into a woman and not apologize. Bill was on time. He told me and Leo, the cinematographer, he had a specific character in mind from this one particular silent film. Neither Leo nor I knew the film, and now I can't remember the title. Bill's performance was very good. During my final edit I knew I needed something to bring the film together, so I asked Bill to read his poem "Melting Milk" as two characters walk away in the end. It's a great scene.

V.

Bill suspects he has a woman's lungs.

VI.

"It's fine to work with loose ends. But they must sparkle or shine."

VII.

I envy Bill's social life. I don't know how he does it. A couple of times he tried to start up a conversation with me about the contemporary music scene, but I hadn't heard any of the bands he was talking about. Now he doesn't bring it up.

VIII.

I was Bill's teacher's assistant during his Lazarus phase. It would take him an extra twenty minutes to get to class because somebody was so surprised to see him alive. Being Bill's assistant was a cakewalk. Everybody is happy to do things for Bill, and he has a natural talent for protocol.

IX.

I've looked at a lot of art with Bill, and a couple of times in the company of his close friends. There's a certain group linked by common experience and uncommon intelligence that I should warn you about. My wife, Erin, and I ran into Bill and a couple of these types in the Met one day. It was intense. The three of them were very casual about the whole thing—just walking around, making observations and tossing around some questions to each other. They were playful, but they demanded a lot from one another. After a couple wings Erin and I were exhausted and headed for the café. They found us. There was a small argument between Bill and George Schnee-man. George wanted museums to keep paintings in the same place, so artists would know where to find them when they needed them. Bill thought they should get out and socialize.

X.

Bill and I recently collaborated with T-shirts. I did some drawings, and he was going to put some words to them. I sent the drawings up to San Francisco from LA. On the phone he told me, "You know we're breaking one of my main rules about collaboration: you got to kind of be in the same place. It makes a difference."

XI.

I met Bill and Connie at their house one day. They had just come from the park, and Bill had lost to Connie in a game of horse. The loss was wearing on him. He explained that it wasn't just losing—it was that he could see the shot so clearly, and the physics refused to follow.

XII.

My wife puts Bill up on a pedestal. She won't go see other poets read any-more because they make her nervous. "When Bill stands up, you know he's got it," she says. So I told her about the students who said Bill's voice would become monotone during lectures. After a pause she shrugged, "He's not a lecturer; he's a poet."

*An uptown, downtown poet or is it a downtown uptown
poet. Then too, as Edwin Denby said of dancers "They
should be pretty" as part of the environment, there is a
look to these poems over the years that's consistent. Also
could live in an elite basket but doesn't and like O'Hara
who accepted life in the cauldron around him, Amazo
New York City, he finds the personal way to allude to and
include the universal.*

—COFFEE HOUSE PRESS, 2008

*"Taste is a sharpened eye for the beautiful, the interesting,
and the unusual—coupled with the talent to apply all of
these to one's life."*
—ELEANOR LAMBERT

Bill Berkson, the poet connected to the painter, the logical descendant of
    Frank O'Hara ("In Memory of My Feelings," O'Hara
and the painters, edited by Berkson). A way of being, really, in the capital
    of the world, New York, the free world at that,
post World War II. Status post the physical manifestation of e = mass times
    the speed of light squared. Perhaps more creature
comfort in landscapes, say the Hudson River School, just up river,
than Rauschenberg, Rivers, de Kooning,
Pollock but then
again not from the standpoint of what you can't see and what you don't
    know when the ultimate powers of the universe
were released on earth in 1945 and 50 years earlier Horsedrawn . . . . . . and
    the temporary beast stalked the Rhine but ultimately
would have been defeated by the cybernetics of the open mind. Thought,
    life as you find it and might make it as a way of being
in art in life . . . . despite being deconstructed by Tom Wolfe as
    arbitrary constructs and value . . . . the open mind with
sight to see. Artists, among their other functions, teach us to see.

So how does poetry fit in here. Words or two around the eye . . . . . eyes.
    Vocabulary to warm the hearth . . . . . . to connect the dots . . .

for a way of life . . . . Fashion too may be an artificial construct but
    taste as in the description of it above can be individualized,
the sine qua non of the New York School of Poets.

In Bill Berkson's new book there is continuity of voice for over forty years.
    Vocabulary and juxtapositions of culture (All Kinds of
Culture) no unexpected precisions in language, sharp turns from various
    knowledge . . . . concern for the human condition
though not exactly political but interpreted through the prism of "taste"
    but not pedestrian . . . . . though knowledgeable of the pedestrian.
An uptown, downtown poet or is it a downtown uptown poet. Then too, as
    Edwin Denby said of dancers "They should be pretty"
as part of the environment, there is a look to these poems over the years
    that's consistent. Also could live in an elite basket but
doesn't and like O'Hara who accepted life in the cauldron around him,
    Amazo New York City, he finds the personal way to allude
to and include the universal.

His lineage as in his poem "Broom Genealogy" is quite interesting and
    thoroughly American . . . . rigor and taste are not hereditary
but are more influenced by environment. French Scotch Irish Dutch . . . .
    A Choctaw a Jew, a huckster or two. A maternal grandfather
who was an advance man for Ringling Bros. and Barnum and Bailey
    Circus. His father who started in journalism on the South Side of
Chicago . . . . . . Capone, Nitti, Leopold and Loeb . . . . . later head of the
    International News Service (I encountered the elder Berkson reading
William Shirer's memoir of the 3rd Reich . . . . he and Shirer sitting in
    Paris in the '30s were trying to arrange an interview with Goebbels)
publisher of the Journal-American in NYC, a now defunct newspaper but
    said this "Get it first, but first get it right." Then of course, his
mother, patriotic grand dame and discoverer, revealer of fashion and talent
    in an elite world who probably never forgot where she came from
(small town Indiana) Eleanor Lambert the author of said Taste quote above.

Billy Berkson, the only poet to have made The International Best Dressed
    List . . . . . hung out at times with poets who had a hard time wearing
matching socks.

Slowed but not bowed by LSMFT (Lucky Strike Makes Fine Tobacco) he
comes out with a book that is a life statement post lung transplant
with all the humiliations of modern medicine, art intact, art sustaining . . . .
. . . . Out on the frontier . . . . They call that True Grit

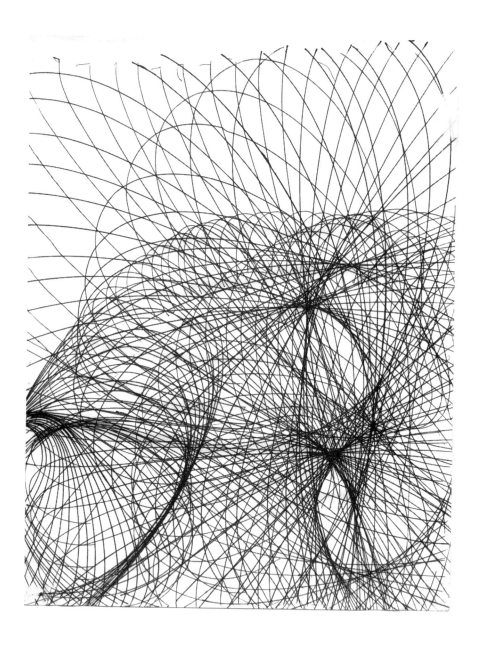

CARLOS VILLA

Bill's second wind / *inhale* / breathtaking!

ANNE WALDMAN

Our Large Algebra

for Bill Berkson

Hinges particularly on enjoyment, the signifier
Purified, the last sip tested or tasted, passion and admiration
Miraculous, a long life parallel in the increments of fun and time
You got grace? You got swing? You got poetry? I got it!
And made a bond, a pact, confessional cab ride, all peoples' desires
We know, sounding mythic through a lens of poetry or art or
Lines with letters connected in a way you hold truce and truth within
Or factorials, studying all operations and relations in a cranium of
Variables, vices and imperfections, gaze out window our slushy metabolic
Streets, carnivalesque sweep of made-up phenomena, breeze at your eye
Whispering love song's long arabesque, o my aria struggling with itself:
Identity & right to be cheeky girl, and you gave that permission, young
Manhattan, possessive one I treasure no squabbling over icons or who
    was he
In Frank O'Hara's marvelous mythology? A muse of course, comrade
As he is that too, all of them Muses a legend, as swank or jazz tone,
Best-dressed and so on, swift wit that too sheds or engages self-propelling
Talk of the instanter upon instanter thought, process for polynomials
Roots *al-jabr* meaning restoration, unmitigated Babylonian task
Consummate brother and to Jim too, asleep by the downtown door
Deep pleasure, pulsing with insight over that line or reticulation a fine eye
Rides that margin of the lake, an old school but quaking modernism,
    stoned
In her boots no *isms* in this body suit, tough aesthete, a supple ersatz
Question what is it you actually *care* about what gives you traction, or
Surprise? surface tension, as New York School rattles the nomenclatures,
And Bolinas shifts the *polis,* cooperative and liberating lagoon
Seizes, describes, never postulates but accosts spanking artificial universe
    from
Sweet Bohemian days, glory and antagonism in shiny speed-demon hour
People and a naturalization of populism, accessible too, charm, harmony
The algebraic equation where you equal my unbridled enthusiasm for

Irrevocable streets, complex avenues, our boulevards, quadruple it and
    people
We can escape to in a re-invocation of multiplicity, place, high talk, poetry
Transcendental imagination, embrace, fabricated movie plots, the planet
Summoning to even greater tasks of love and valor, get ready

LEWIS WARSH

DARK STUDY

for Bill Berkson

There's something we don't know about that's happening
    elsewhere

A photo by Weegee of a corpse on the streets of Paris

An emergency call from the school nurse went unheeded

All my belongings in one suitcase—how can I help you today?

Add *-er* to an adjective when you're comparing two objects
    or people

It looks good on the page but when you read it aloud something
    goes wrong

Matches used once may be bartered for tallow

We can trade identities for a few hours & you can feel
    what it's like to be me

You can take the initiative and lean out the window
    until your hair touches the sidewalk or you can
    build a moat around yourself & never touch
    bottom

Maybe abstraction sounds the deathknell to the colloquial
    stammer, a tightening of the windpipe as the muffler
    explodes

A boat passing under a bridge or a woman kneeling
    at the edge of the shore

The cars passing in the opposite direction dim their lights
    when they see me coming

Possibly you can forget about your own needs for the moment

Maybe I have a brain inside my head afterall

We go to bed early & wake with the sun

The sun comes through the curtains like the plague,
    & we open our eyes

I slammed the door, boarded the subway, & never looked back

I crossed out what you said before you said it, without
    thinking twice

The cranberry juice left a stain on the sheet

All new arrivals are cautioned to stay indoors after dark

They built the boardwalk so the old people can sit in the sun,
    but when the sun goes down everyone & their mother
    disappears

A minute feels like an hour, a day is longer than a year

You better turn on the defroster if you want to see through
    the windshield

The animal fled into the woods on the other side of the road

Patches of ice float down the windshield in slow motion

All the shadings (equanimity, desire, abandonment)
    that never add up

Half-sentences mixed with half-truths, complacency
 and error—is that your real hair?

It doesn't matter where you were born or where you were going

The suspect climbs down the fire escape & disappears through
 a hole in the floor

Someone too drunk to remember stumbles by under
 your window

It was before the days of radio & everyone played their own
 music

Some poets went to brothels, caught diseases, eventually died

Step back from the path & look at yourself, feigning innocence

Turn your back on the javelin while it's still in the air

If I had a hammer it would work both ways, from the center
 to the interior, & out into the open

"But there are no more jobs in the city—we must return home
 to the countryside"

It's her word against mine (if only the trees could speak)

We walk through a cemetery & read the names on the stones

A horse is like a large dog, but with different habits

Memory lingers on, but the distinguishing marks are a blur

The party isn't even half-over & already numerous guests
 have passed out on the living room rug

What you wanted was right in front of your eyes,
    but you didn't see it

It's hard to know what you want when something's being given
    to you

You can see your whole life pass in front of you in a few
    minutes

The milkman comes to the door in a horror movie from the 1950s
    but no one's home

We park the car at the end of the cul-de-sac & listen
    to the birds on the top branches, while the songs
    on the radio curdle around us in the stillness

They came to my door with a warrant, but they didn't find anything

They looked under the bed but all they found were a few ghosts

There are tears running down the face of the statue

Rain falls on our eyelids, but we don't wake up

It's a long pilgrimage into the bowels of the earth until you hit
    rock bottom

It was like a miracle to see the statue of the Virgin Mary
    shedding tears

You never know who you might meet when you walk
    down the street

Pride is the same as desire, on a different planet

I'd like to write an epiphany to the saints, but who are they?

Midge, Molly, Maggie, Mickey & Marge

RICHARD WENTWORTH

A Free Man

This week, I put some overnight essentials into a plastic bag—passport, shaving things, tickets, a pictorial lecture on a CD, two books.

I hesitated over my bunch of house keys and hung them up above the kettle.

Closing the front door, locking the mortise with the spare key, I tossed it through the letter box, simultaneously realizing that my mobile phone was on charge inside.

The warm sunshine and the marvelous sensation of isolation, of being unplugged, an instant orphan, swept over me. No telephone numbers in my memory, that instantaneous sense of disembodiment, which has now become such an exception to the human rule.

Like Bill, I come from the twentieth century, and we met by chance encounter on the hinge of two centuries.

On the 13th of September, 2001, Bill offered me a ride from San Francisco across the bay to Berkeley to hear Martin Puryear speak.

The rude engineering of the bridge and the density of post–September 11th commuter traffic was a novelty to me.

Bill and I talked shyly about who we were.

He described vividly his own birth, his mother going into labor in a New York hospital, with the sound of a radio on, much too loud, carrying the news of Hitler's invasion of Poland.

His mother, said Bill, shouted to the nurse to turn down the radio.

The nurse, said Bill, shouted back to his mother, "Don't you want to hear the news?"

There are odd moments in lives when the comforting feeling of suspension (of belief, as much as physical weightlessness) make fine memories.

The ride with Bill on the bridge was one of those.

KYLE SCHLESINGER

Big Sky Books and Big Sky *Magazine*

Between Christmas and New Year's 1969–70, Bill Berkson visited Tom Clark and fellow New York native Lewis Warsh in Bolinas, a relatively secluded beach community approximately thirty miles north of San Francisco. It was his first time there. In '69, Clark and Warsh had published their collaboration *Chicago* (Angel Hair) out of Bolinas, and in '70 they co-edited *Sugar Mountain,* a one-shot magazine with a beautiful photograph of Alice Notley on the cover. These were two of the early poetry publications from the heyday of the Bolinas poetry scene that lasted from the late sixties to the mid-seventies. New York poets Ted Berrigan and Notley were also visiting Bolinas that winter. Berkson had already published his first book of poems, *Saturday Night: Poems, 1960–1961* (Tibor de Nagy, 1961) and written collaborations with Frank O'Hara, and his book *Shining Leaves* with a gorgeous cover by Alex Katz had just been published by Warsh and Anne Waldman's Angel Hair Books. At age thirty-one, the poet made a decision to move from New York City, his hometown, to Bolinas. Who would have imagined that the young city slicker would live there for twenty-three years? Not Bill.

Just before leaving New York, Berkson edited and published his first one-shot magazine, *Best & Company,* which included work by Ted Berrigan, Frank O'Hara, Joe Brainard, William Burroughs, and many more. In the late spring of 1970, Berkson, Jim Carroll, and Jim's then-girlfriend Devereaux Carson drove cross-country from New York to Bolinas in a rented car. Kevin Opstedal tells the story well in his article "Dreaming as One" in the online magazine *Big Bridge.* In addition to Warsh and Clark, Joanne Kyger, John Thorpe, Bill Brown, and Ebbe Borregaard were already there, and within a few years Robert Creeley, Lewis MacAdams, Robert Grenier, Aram Saroyan, Michael Wolfe, Donald Allen, Philip Whalen, Jim Brodey, Jim Gustafson, Tom Veitch, Grace Slick & Marty Balin, Stephen Ratcliffe, Arthur Okamura, Duncan McNaughton, and other writers and artists had settled there as well.

Although he had grown up at the center of the publishing universe, it wasn't until he got to Bolinas that Berkson established what was to become one of the most significant of the adventurous small presses of the golden era of publishing in America. Between 1971 and 1978, Berkson edited and published at least twenty Big Sky books as well as twelve substantial issues of *Big Sky* magazine. In *A Secret Location on the Lower East Side*, Berkson reflects on Big Sky: "Joe Brainard's *Bolinas Journal* was the first Big Sky book, soon followed by *The Cargo Cult* by John Thorpe. The name was suggested by Tom Veitch, who lived around the lagoon, in Stinson Beach, and who reminded me of the line from a Kinks song, 'Big Sky looks down on all the people . . . .'" Before the digital age of internet and email, letters and magazines were the way news traveled from coast to coast. Each issue of *Big Sky* was longer than the one that had preceded it, and the magazine culminated with a book-length double issue entitled "Homage to Frank O'Hara," co-edited by Berkson and Joe LeSueur in April 1978. *Big Sky* wasn't as ephemeral as other magazines of the mimeo era; each issue was carefully edited, typeset, and saddle-stapled (the last two issues perfect-bound), while many other magazines were more whimsical in their material and editorial composition. *Big Sky* made cordial introductions and provided a means to keep up the conversation among his friends on both coasts. There was no advertising and no submissions policy. Reading through all of the issues, there is clearly a core group of contributors, some of whom also published books with Big Sky.

Of the books published, approximately two-thirds of the artists and writers were based in New York (Joe Brainard, Larry Fagin, Anne Waldman, Alice Notley, Alex Katz, Ted Greenwald, Richard Nonas, George Schneeman, Ron Padgett, Bernadette Mayer, Jim Brodey, Yvonne Jacquette, and Ed Bowes) while others were based in California (Joanne Kyger, Michael Myers, John Thorpe, Greg Irons, and Jim Gustafson).

A few of the books, such as David Anderson's *The Spade in the Sensorium* and Jim Gustafson's *Tales of Virtue and Transformation*, were issued in classic mimeograph format: letter-size, black-and-white, and side-stapled. Editions ranged from 200 to 1,500 copies (about the same as any small press specializing in poetry today). The majority of the books were printed offset and either perfect-bound or saddle-stapled. Well made and carefully conceived, the books were entirely devoid of pretense, although there was usually a "special edition" of twenty-six copies, identical to the trade edition, that were numbered or lettered and signed by the poet and the artist. Although Richard Nixon has not been historicized as a great supporter of the arts, it's worth noting that the National Endowment for the Arts and

Coordinating Council of Literary Magazines grants flourished under his administration (1969–74), providing many young artists, publishers, and writers the opportunity to bring challenging new writing into print. (As Berkson himself notes, some publishers of that time arguably exploited the funding and produced books in excessive and/or extravagant editions.) Berkson learned the nuances of making copperplates for offset printing and the art of preparing camera-ready copy. He notes:

> With *Big Sky* 4 — bearing its great wrap-around Philip Guston cover and especially powerful contributions by Creeley, Ron Padgett, and Bernadette Mayer — I hit my stride as editor. Six years later, having published twelve issues of the magazine and more than twenty books, I decided I'd done the job.

.   .   .

This is a checklist of Big Sky Books and *Big Sky* magazine, both edited and published by poet and critic Bill Berkson in Bolinas, California. The press produced some ephemera; these are not included in this checklist because they are, by definition, inherently difficult to find, but records indicate that Big Sky published at least two items: a broadside by Clark Coolidge entitled "Moroccan Variations" in 1971 and a postcard by Lewis MacAdams entitled "I Have Been Tested and Found Not Insane" in 1974. Sorted chronologically by year, each item is listed with its dimensions, height preceding width, in inches. Most titles were printed on offset presses and saddled-stapled or perfect-bound, with one-, two-, or three-color covers; a few were printed letterpress or on a mimeograph machine. Retail prices are noted when they appear on the cover. A few books were produced in conjunction with Larry Fagin's *Adventures in Poetry* in New York City. Special thanks to: Jim Maynard at the Poetry Collection of the University Libraries, University at Buffalo, the State University of New York, for scanning Bill Berkson's *Terrace Fence*; Molly Schwartzburg at the Harry Ransom Center, University of Texas at Austin, for her assistance and for allowing me to examine Steve Carey's *Gentle Subsidy*; Wendy Burk of the Poetry Collection at the University of Arizona for visiting the Special Collections Library to make a record of Anne Waldman's *Spin Off*; and, of course, poet, publisher, critic, curator, and friend Bill Berkson for making all of these possibilities possible.

NOTE: *All measurements given in inches, height preceding width*

1971 · [1] *Bolinas Journal*
Joe Brainard
11 × 8.5; 50 pp. Cover and drawings throughout by the author, as well as holographs of poems by Ted Berrigan and Anne Waldman and a drawing of the author by Philip Whalen. Published in an edition of 300 copies, of which 26 "special" copies are lettered A to Z and signed by the author. Text pages printed at The Press by Mickey Cummings. Cover printed at the Rip Off Press in San Francisco. Black-and-white cover, side-stapled. Bolinas, California.

[2] *Two Serious Poems & One Other*
Bill Berkson & Larry Fagin
8 × 6; 12 pp. Cover by Joe Brainard. Published in an edition of 200 copies, of which 10 are numbered and signed by the authors. Two-color cover, saddle-stapled. Bolinas, California.

[3] *Terrace Fence*
Bill Berkson
8.5 × 5.5; 12 pp. Cover by the author. Edition not stated. A book of photographs printed rectos only, two back-and-white pictures of fence and sea per page. Includes handwritten title page and colophon. Saddle-stapled. Bolinas, California.

1972 · [4] *Spin Off*
Anne Waldman
11 × 8.5; 20 pp. Published in an edition of 200 free copies by Big Sky. Facsimile of handwritten text with line drawings. Black-and-white cover, side-stapled. Bolinas, California.

[5] *The Cargo Cult*
John Thorpe
10 × 7; 112 pp. Cover photograph by Keith Dennison courtesy of the *Oakland Tribune*. Title page rendering of cover photograph by Michael Myers.

Published in an edition of 1,000 copies. Printed at Globe Printing Company in San Jose, California. Composition by Spring Creek in Linotype Cloister. Bolinas, California.

1973 · [6] *Phoebe Light*
Alice Notley
9.5 × 6.5; 40 pp. Cover by Alex Katz. Published in an edition of 750 copies, of which 26 copies are numbered and signed by the poet and the artist. Printed at Grape Press in San Francisco. Black-and-white cover, saddled-stapled. Bolinas, California.

1974 · [7] *The Spade in the Sensorium*
David Anderson
8.5 × 11; 40 pp. Cover by Philip Guston. Published in an edition of 600 copies. Printed at the Mesa Press, Bolinas. Black-and-white cover, side-stapled. Bolinas, California.

[8] *The Life*
Ted Greenwald
9.5 × 6.5; 40 pp. Cover by Richard Nonas. Published in an edition of 750 copies, of which 26 copies are numbered and signed by the poet and the artist. Printed at the Mesa Press, Bolinas. Black-and-white cover, saddle-stapled. Bolinas, California.

[9] *Crazy Compositions*
Ron Padgett
9.5 × 6.5; 24 pp. Cover by George Schneeman. Published in an edition of 750 copies at the Mesa Press, Bolinas, of which 26 copies are lettered A to Z and signed by the poet and the artist. Printed and produced at Grape Press, San Francisco. Two-color cover, saddle-stapled. Bolinas, California.

[10] *Tales of Virtue and Transformation*
Jim Gustafson
11 × 8.5; 44 pp. Cover by Greg Irons. Published in an edition of 600 copies, of which 26 are lettered A to Z and signed by the poet and the artist. Black-and-white cover, side-stapled. Bolinas, California.

1975 · [11] *Polaroid*
Clark Coolidge

9 × 6; 104 pp. $3. Published with *Adventures in Poetry* in an edition of 1,000 copies, of which 26 are lettered A to Z and signed by the poet. Distributed by Serendipity Books. Two-color cover, black endpapers, perfect-bound. Bolinas, California, and New York City.

[12] *Blues of the Egyptian Kings (1962–1975)*
Jim Brodey

9 × 6; 136 pp. $4. Cover by Greg Irons. "Brodey Notes" by Clark Coolidge printed on inside front and rear covers. Published in an edition of 1,000 copies, of which 26 are lettered A to Z and signed by the poet and the artist. Distributed by Serendipity Books. Three-color cover, with author photo in blue and pink on the back by James Hamilton, red endpapers, perfect-bound. Bolinas, California.

[13] *Studying Hunger*
Bernadette Mayer

10 × 8; 72 pp. $3. Cover photograph by Ed Bowes. Published with Adventures in Poetry in an edition of 1,000 copies, of which 26 are lettered A to Z and signed by the poet. Distributed by Serendipity Books. Black-and-white cover, perfect-bound. Bolinas, California, and New York City.

[14] *All This Every Day*
Joanne Kyger

9 × 6; 96 pp. $4. Cover photograph by Francesco Pellizzi. Cover and title page composition by Zephyrus Image. Published in an edition of 1,500 copies, of which 26 are lettered A to Z and signed by the poet. Distributed by Serendipity Books. Two-color cover, perfect-bound. Bolinas, California.

[15] *Enigma Variations*
Bill Berkson

9 × 6; 48 pp. Cover and 16 drawings by Philip Guston. Published in an edition of 1,000 copies, of which 26 are lettered A to Z and signed by the poet and the artist. Distributed by Serendipity Books. Black-and-white cover, orange endpapers, perfect-bound. Bolinas, California.

[16] *Gentle Subsidy*
Steve Carey
9 × 6; 64 pp. Cover by Effie Rosen. Published in an edition of 600 copies, of which 26 are lettered A to Z and signed by the poet. Black ink on blue paper, perfect-bound. Bolinas, California.

[17] *Opera—Works*
Barrett Watten
7.75 × 5.5; 64 pp. $2.50. Cover photographs by the author. Published in an edition of 600 copies, of which 26 are lettered A to Z and signed by the poet. Printed at the West Coast Print Center. Distributed by Serendipity Books. Two-color cover, saddle-stapled. Bolinas, California.

1976 · [18] *Above the Treeline*
Dick Gallup
9 × 6; 64 pp. Cover by Yvonne Jacquette. Published in an edition of 750 copies, of which 26 are lettered A to Z and signed by the poet. Distributed by Serendipity Books. Two-color cover, perfect-bound. Bolinas, California.

[19] *Seven Poems*
Larry Fagin
5.75 × 7.25; 16 pp. Published in an edition of 300 copies, of which 26 are lettered A to Z and signed by the poet. Printed and designed by Wesley B. Tanner in Berkeley. Distributed by Serendipity Books. Two-color cover, pamphlet-sewn. Bolinas, California.

[20] *Death College & Other Poems (1964–1974)*
Tom Veitch
9 × 6; 184 pp. Afterword by Allen Ginsberg. Cover photo by Martha Veitch. Includes illustrations by Tom Veitch, Dick Gallup, Joe Brainard, George Schneeman, and others. Published in an edition of 1,500 copies, of which 26 are lettered A to Z and signed by the poet. Distributed by Serendipity Books. Two-color cover, perfect-bound. Bolinas, California.

Big Sky, no. 1, 1971

10 × 7; 80 pp. Two-color cover by Gregg Irons. Saddle-stapled. Contributors: Alice Notley, Michael Brownstein, Ted Berrigan, Robert Creeley, Harris Schiff, Tom Veitch, Lewis Warsh, Charlie Vermont, Diane di Prima, David Rosenberg, Tom Clark, Anne Waldman, Lewis MacAdams, Grant Fisher, Clark Coolidge, Hilton Obenzinger, Joanne Kyger, Bill Berkson, Greg Irons, John Thorpe, Bobbie Creeley, Joe Brainard, Philip Whalen, Alan Senauke, Kenward Elmslie, Allen Ginsberg, and Scott Cohen. Art by Arthur Okamura.

Big Sky, no. 2, 1972

10 × 7; 80 pp. Black-and-white cover by Alex Katz. Saddle-stapled. Contributors include: Allen Ginsberg, John Thorpe, Dick Gallup, Andrew Baldwin, Diane di Prima, Robert Creeley, Joe Brainard, James Schuyler, Harry Mathews, Ebbe Borregaard, Hilton Obenzinger, Charlie Walsh, Philip Whalen, Ted Berrigan, Andrei Codrescu, Kenward Elmslie, Alan Senauke, Lewis MacAdams, Ron Padgett, John Giorno, Charlie Vermont, Anne Waldman, Tom Clark, Clark Coolidge, Michael Brownstein, Bill Berkson, Larry Fagin, Scott Cohen, Tom Veitch, Alice Notley, Joanne Kyger, and Lewis Warsh. Art by Louis Aragon, Greg Irons, Gordon Baldwin, and Darrell DeVore.

Big Sky, no. 3, 1972

9.85 × 6.85; 76 pp. Black-and-white cover by Celia Elizabeth Coolidge. Saddle-stapled. This issue is comprised entirely of previously unpublished poetry by Clark Coolidge. Introduction by Tom Clark.

Big Sky, no. 4, 1972

10 × 7; 84 pp. Black-and-white cover by Philip Guston. Saddle-stapled. Contributors include: Bernadette Mayer, David Meltzer, Ron Padgett, Marty McClain, Jim Brodey & Terry Allen, Robert Creeley, Anselm Hollo, Peter Schjeldahl, Philip Guston, Clark Coolidge, David Antin, Tom Clark, Hilton Obenzinger, Andrei Codrescu, Joe Brainard, and Aram Saroyan. Art by Tom Clark, Greg Irons, and Joe Brainard.

Big Sky, no. 5, 1973

9.75 × 7; 88 pp. Blue-and-white cover by George Schneeman. Saddle-stapled. Contributors include: Joanne Kyger, Johnny Stanton, Tom Raworth, James Schuyler, John Wieners, Philip Guston, Lewis Warsh, Bill Berkson & Joanne Kyger, Bill Berkson, Aram Saroyan, Hilton Obenzinger, Lewis Warsh, Michael Brownstein, Tom Clark, Jim Gustafson, Lawrence Ferling-hetti, Gerard Malanga, Ted Greenwald, Anne Waldman, Lewis MacAdams, Tom Veitch, and Larry Fagin. Art by Johnny Stanton, Philip Guston, Arthur Okamura, Bill Berkson, Tom Clark, and Joe Brainard.

Big Sky, no. 6, 1973

9.75 × 6.75; 132 pp. Two-color cover by Norman Bluhm. Saddle-stapled. Printed at the San Francisco Community Press and typeset by Tom Veitch. Double issue. Contributors include: Ted Greenwald, Michael Brownstein, Harris Schiff, Tony Towle, John Godfrey, Dick Gallup, Johnny Stanton, James Schuyler, Barrett Watten, Ron Padgett, Rudy Burckhardt, Edwin Denby, Curtis Faville, Kenward Elmslie, Anne Waldman, David Anderson, Fielding Dawson, Lewis Warsh, Charlie Vermont, Hilton Obenzinger, Jim Gustafson, Larry Fagin, Clark Coolidge, Tom Veitch, Aram Saroyan, and Bill Berkson. Collaborative watercolor, *Ear,* by Bill Berkson, Tom Clark, and George Schneeman.

Big Sky, no. 7, 1974

9.75 × 6.75; 48 pp. Black-and-white cover by Leon. Saddle-stapled. This issue is comprised entirely of previously unpublished poetry by Leon. Introduction by Donald Hall.

Big Sky, no. 8, 1974

10.25 × 7.125; 112 pp. Green-and-white cover by Joe Brainard. Saddle-stapled. Printed at Apex Novelties in San Francisco and typeset by Barrett Watten. Contributors include: Anne Waldman & George Schneeman, Bill Berkson, Frank O'Hara, Bobbie Louise Hawkins, Jim Carroll, Rebecca Brown, Lewis MacAdams, Clark Coolidge, Michael Brownstein, Ted Berrigan, John Ashbery, Lewis Warsh, Ron Padgett, Ted Greenwald, Tom Clark, Joanne Kyger, Jim Carroll, Harry Mathews, Alice Notley, Ken Mikolowski, Robert Creeley, John Godfrey, and Steve Carey. Art by Tom Clark and John Gruen.

Big Sky, no. 9, 1975

10.15 × 7; 150 pp. Black-and-white cover by Red Grooms. Perfect-bound. Printed at the West Coast Print Center and typeset by Barrett Watten. Contributors include: Giorgio de Chirico, Philip Whalen, Joseph Ceravolo, Kenneth Koch, Vladimir Mayakovsky, Jim Carroll, Bernadette Mayer, Anne Waldman, William Corbett, Kenward Elmslie, John Godfrey, James Schuyler, Frank O'Hara, Lorenzo Thomas, Ed Sanders, Carl Rakosi, Jim Gustafson, Ron Padgett & George Schneeman, Ron Padgett, Michael Palmer, Barrett Watten, James Schuyler, John Thorpe, Jim Brodey, Tom Veitch, Bill Berkson, Bobbie Louise Hawkins, Lewis Warsh, Terrence Winch, Charles Reznikoff, Peter Schjeldahl, Joanne Kyger, Ted Greenwald, Tom Raworth, Simon Schuchat, Curtis Faville, Ted Berrigan, Alice Notley, and Clark Coolidge. Art by Philip Guston. Photograph of Frank O'Hara & James Schuyler by John Button, 1952.

Big Sky, no. 10, 1976

10 × 7; 144 pp. $2.50. Black-and-white cover by Gordon Baldwin. Perfect-bound. Printed at the West Coast Print Center and typeset by Barrett Watten. Contributors include: Clark Coolidge, Federico Garcia Lorca, Jamie MacInnis, Lisa Nunez, Summer Brenner, Rudy Burckhardt, Kenneth Rexroth, Bill Berkson, Gordon Baldwin, Ronald Johnson, Keith Abbott, Kit Robinson, Bob Perelman, Philip Whalen, Lewis MacAdams, Alan Davies, Henry Kanabus, Fielding Dawson, Philippe Soupault, Ted Greenwald, Steve Carey, Maureen Owen, Allen Ginsberg, and Merrill Gilfillan. Drawings for "Sorroche in Peru" by Red Grooms and Mimi Gross.

Big Sky, nos. 11 & 12, originally published in 1978 [reprinted 1988]

10 × 7; 224 pp. $12. Edited by Bill Berkson and Joe LeSueur. Black-and-white cover by Jane Frelicher. Perfect-bound. Editors' note by Bill Berkson and Joe LeSueur. Contributors include: Willem de Kooning, Kenward Elmslie, Anne Waldman, Ted Berrigan, Morton Feldman, John Ciardi, John Ashbery, Jane Freilicher, Lawrence Osgood, Kenneth Koch, Walter Silver, John Bernard Myers, Ned Rorem, John Button, Joe LeSueur, Larry Rivers & Frank O'Hara, Robert Duncan & Allen Ginsberg, John Wieners, Philip Whalen, Robert Creeley, Fred W. McDarrah, Vincent Warren, Barbara Guest, Irving Sandler, Jean Dubuffet, James Schuyler, Waldo Rasmussen, Renee S. Neu, Alice Neel, Elaine de Kooning, Alex Katz, Philip

Guston, Jack Larson, Joe Brainard & Frank O'Hara, Terry Southern, Mario Schifano, Patsy Southgate, Michael Goldberg & Frank O'Hara, Norman Bluhm & Frank O'Hara, Ruth Krauss, Ron Padgett, James Schuyler, Larry Rivers, Peter Schjeldahl, J. J. Mitchell, Lewis MacAdams, Aram Saroyan, David Shapiro, Tony Towle, Patsy Southgate, Jim Brodey, Diane di Prima, Allan Kaplan, Vincent Katz, Bill Berkson, Joe Brainard, Erje Ayden, Edmund Leites, Charles Olson, Gerard Malanga, Ted Greenwald, John Cage, Clark Coolidge, Imamu Amiri Baraka, James Schuyler, Jim Gustafson, Stephen Rodefer, Paul Schmidt, Susan Friedland, Bruce Boone, Kenneth Koch, Simon Schuchat, Transcripts of *USA*.

A Selection of Covers

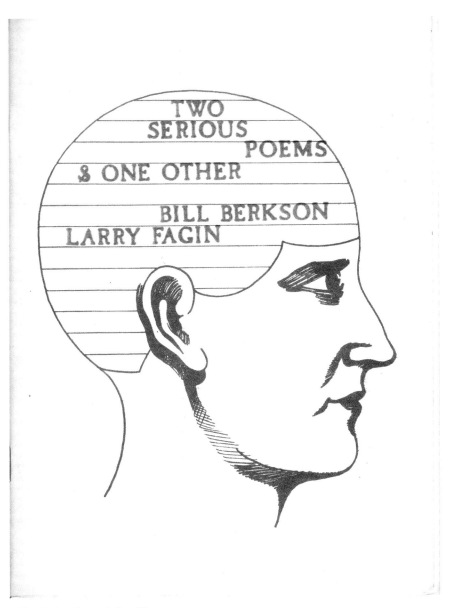

2. Two Serious Poems & One Other

5. *The Cargo Cult*

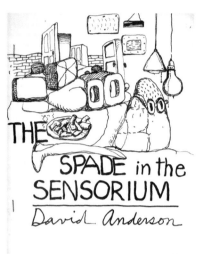

7. *The Spade in the Sensorium*

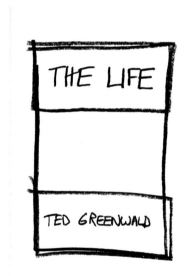

8. *The Life*

9. *Crazy Compositions*

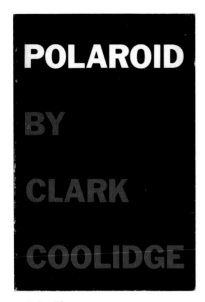

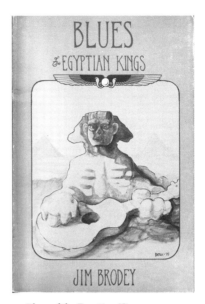

11. *Polaroid*   12. *Blues of the Egyptian Kings*

13. *Studying Hunger*   14. *All This Every Day*

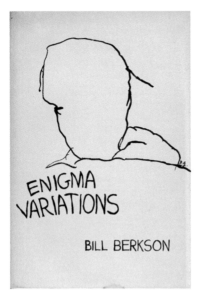

15. *Enigma Variations*

17. *Opera—Works*

18. *Above the Treeline*

19. *Seven Poems*

20. *Death College & Other Poems*

Big Sky, no. 1

Big Sky, no. 2

Big Sky, no. 3

Big Sky, no. 4

Big Sky, no. 5

Big Sky, no. 6

Big Sky, no. 7

Big Sky, no. 8

Big Sky, no. 9

Big Sky, no. 10

Big Sky, nos. 11 and 12

COLTER JACOBSEN

A postcard that I sent Bill and I don't think he ever received it. I'm happy that I took a picture of it. It has the butterfly and the double-B's back to back. Whenever I see butterflies, I think of Bill's beautiful collage/collab between O'Hara and BRAINard. It depicts a butterfly with a thought bubble that reads, "I'm not really flying, I'm thinking." Always a favorite of mine. And the butterfly makes me think of Bill's lungs, for which we are all so grateful.

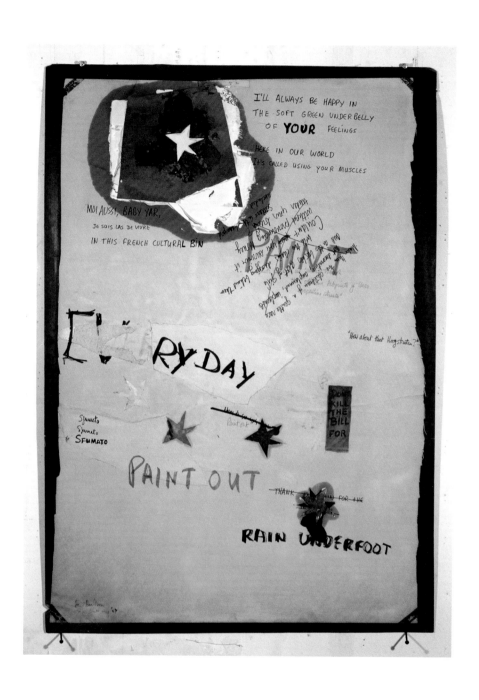

MICHAEL GOLDBERG   collaboration with Bill Berkson; 1964

LEONIE GUYER

down at the box-office
of Town Hall I was thinking
of you in your no hat
music often reminds me
of nothing, that way,
like reforming —

Frank
10/7/61

FRANK O'HARA

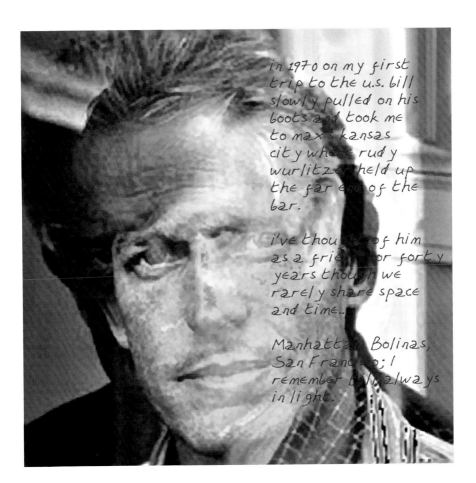

in 1970 on my first
trip to the u.s. bill
slowly pulled on his
boots and took me
to max kansas
city where rudy
wurlitzer held up
the far end of the
bar.

i've thought of him
as a friend for forty
years though we
rarely share space
and time.

Manhattan, Bolinas,
San Francisco; I
remember bill always
in light.

TOM RAWORTH

BILL... IN THE EXTREMELY EXTREMELY, EXTREMELY REMOTE POSSIBILITY THAT YOU
WOULD EVER TITLE ONE OF YOUR BOOKS "GOODS & SERVICES", THEN THIS COULD BE
USED AS THE COVER - BEST TO YOU! Ed Ruscha

ED RUSCHA

GEORGE SCHNEEMAN

GEORGE SCHNEEMAN   collaboration with Bill Berkson; 2008

Stars fell
empty handed

Now the sky feels
The gods must love you
so

collaboration with Bill Berkson; 2007

ISABELLE SORRELL

In The Breeze

Buddhism says it is possible to get your
mind together like the wings of a butterfly.
It is also possible not to get your mind
together and still exist like a butterfly
but with no wings.

GEORGE SCHNEEMAN

ANNE WALDMAN

I Can Write

little recital

bent over the spoon

move motion to

the kernel

fluent impossible worlds

stars to wave to

"hello" and

"I follow your obsession"

alone, cool and shining

[for Bill]

TREVOR WINKFIELD

JOHN ZURIER

PHONG BUI